THE
NORMAN
CONQUESTS

A Trilogy of Plays

ALAN AYCKBOURN

GROVE PRESS, INC.
NEW YORK

First Black Cat Edition 1979
First Printing 1979
ISBN: 0-394-17082-2
Grove Press ISBN: 0-8021-4243-5
Library of Congress Catalog Card Number: 78-73051

LIBRARY OF CONGRESS CATALOGING IN PUBLICATION DATA

Ayckbourn, Alan, 1939—
The Norman conquests.

Reprint of the ed. published by Chatto and Windus, London.

CONTENTS: Table manner.—Living together.—Round and
round the garden.
I. Title
PR6051.Y35N6 1979   822′.9′14   78-73501
ISBN 0-394-17082-2 (Random House)

Manufactured in the United States of America

Distributed by Random House, Inc. New York
GROVE PRESS, INC., 196 West Houston Street,
New York, N.Y. 10014

First produced at the Library Theatre, Scarborough in June 1973 and subsequently at the Greenwich Theatre in May 1974. West End production presented by Michael Codron at the Globe Theatre, London on 1 August 1974 with the following cast:

NORMAN	TOM COURTENAY
TOM	MICHAEL GAMBON
SARAH	PENELOPE KEITH
ANNIE	FELICITY KENDAL
REG	MARK KINGSTON
RUTH	BRIDGET TURNER

Directed by Eric Thompson
Designed by Alan Pickford

Contents

PREFACE

In general, by an odd quirk of nature, the more fond of
people I become, the more amusing I tend to find them.
Love affairs in my life are matters of considerable hilarity.
Necessarily, this has strictly curtailed not only my close
circle of friends but my choice of female companions. Few
women care to be laughed at and men not at all, except for
large sums of money. All of which leads to the fact that I'm
far too fond of the theatre to take it too seriously.

This preface is not intended to enlarge upon or in any
way illuminate the plays contained in this volume. Despite
notable exceptions, playwrights who attempt such com-
ments are prone at best to sound faintly pretentious or
(worse) untypically modest.

The Norman Conquests are the result of several days and
nights of almost continuous writing in the spring of 1973.
Already, little over a year later, it's difficult for me to
remember why I chose to tackle this most ambitious and,
frankly, seemingly uncommercial project. I think it was,
within the context of the tiny Library Theatre-in-the-
Round in Scarborough where I first stage all my plays,
both a challenge and something of an adventure for the
actors and for me as director. Certainly I never dreamed
they would be produced elsewhere. Trilogies, I was in-
formed by my London sources as soon as the news leaked
out that I was writing one, are not Good Things for the
West End. But then, when I am tackling a new play, I find
it safer never to look further than Scarborough anyway. It
always seems at the time quite enough of an effort to write
and stage the play and achieve success there. Afterwards,
when perhaps the piece is run in and seems to be working,
it becomes possible to be objective and consider its chances
elsewhere. In this I have always been extremely fortunate.
I have written, to date, fifteen full-length plays, most of
which are happily destroyed, but all without exception,
even the first, guaranteed production before I set pencil to

paper. In latter years, this apparent blind and some would say foolish faith that the management of Scarborough seemed to have that I would always produce the work is explained by the fact that I am also the Theatre's Artistic Director. Like most successful relationships, this one is based on implicit mutual trust. All of which, I suppose, goes a long way to explain why I continue to work there and not, as has been suggested to me, try for the "big time".

Of course, this system has its restrictions, but fortunately these too seem to work in my favour. Scarborough is a holiday town, which means that a large proportion of the potential audience changes every week of the summer. On Saturdays, the roads in and out of the town are scenes of mile-long queues as visitors leave and arrive. When I first considered the trilogy, I was aware that it would be optimistic to expect an audience like this necessarily to be able to give up three nights of their precious holiday to come to our one theatre. Any suggestion that it was essential to see all three plays to appreciate any one of them would probably result in no audience at all. Similarly, were the plays clearly labelled Parts One, Two and Three, any holidaymaker determined to play Bingo on Monday would probably give up the whole idea as a bad job. The plays would therefore have to be able to stand independently— yet not so much that people's curiosity as to what was happening on the other two nights wasn't a little aroused. Second, as I have said, it should be possible to see them in any order. Third, since we could only afford six actors, they should have that number of characters. Fourth, ideally they should only have two stage entrances since that's the way our temporary Library Theatre set-up is arranged (but then this is common to all my plays). There were other minor pre-conditions peculiar to this venture. The actor I had in mind to play Norman couldn't join us for the first few days of the season—which necessitated him making a late first entrance in one of the plays (*Table Manners*) to facilitate rehearsals. If this all makes me sound like a writer

who performs to order, I suppose it's true. I thrive when
working under a series of pre-conditions, preferably when
they are pre-conditions over which I have total control.
Because ultimately, of course, all these restrictions that
come as a result of operating in a converted concert room,
a temporary 250-seat Theatre-in-the-Round on the first
floor of a public library, tend to work in a play's favour in
its later life. In these austere times most theatre managers,
if not the actors, prefer small-cast plays. Owing to our
scenic restrictions, they are also amenable to plays with
simple sets and, in the case of the trilogy, its flexibility of
presentation has naturally proved an advantage elsewhere.
The traffic jams of visitors to Heathrow are no less than the
ones to Scarborough.

Anyway, once I had sorted out the pre-conditions and
was aware that the scheme had few precedents, the problem
of how to write it arose. I'm not one of those careful,
methodic over-all planners. When I start a play, beyond
an entirely general pattern, I have little or no idea what
will become of my characters individually at the end. I
generally follow their progress with a more or less benign
interest and hope that the staging and construction will
be taken care of by some divine subconscious automatic
pilot. Since many of the actions within the plays had to
cross-relate and, more important, since each character's
attitude and development had to fit in with the general time
structure, I decided in the case of *The Norman Conquests* to
write them crosswise. That is to say, I started with Scene
One of *Round And Round The Garden*, then the Scene One's
of the other two plays and so on through the Scene Two's.
It was an odd experience writing them, rather similar to
Norman's own in fact. I found myself grappling with triplet
sisters all with very different personalities. Climaxes, comic
ones naturally, seemed to abound everywhere. Hardly had I
finished dealing with the fury of Reg's game (*Living
Together*) than I was encountering a frenzied Sarah trying
to seat her guests (*Table Manners*) or Ruth beating off the

advances of an uncharacteristically amorous Tom (*Round and Round The Garden*). Strangely too, each play, although dealing with the same characters and events, began to develop a distinct atmosphere of its own. *Table Manners* was the most robust and, as it proved onstage, the most overtly funny. *Round and Round The Garden*, possibly due to its exterior setting, took a more casual and (as it contains the beginning and end of the cycle) a more conventional shape. *Living Together* has a tempo far slower than anything I had written before and encouraged me, possibly because of the sheer over-all volume of writing involved, to slacken the pace in a way I had never dared to do in any comedy. This crosswise way of writing them proved very satisfactory though of course made it quite impossible for me, even today, really to judge their effectiveness downwards or indeed to assess, beyond certain limits, whether the plays stand up independently. This is not, I'm afraid, a problem that one single individual can resolve. As soon as one play is read or seen, the other two plays are automatically coloured and affected by the foreknowledge gained from the first—which may sound like some sort of warning, though, in this case I hope, a little knowledge is a pleasurable thing.

ALAN AYCKBOURN
Scarborough 1974

THE NORMAN CONQUESTS

TABLE MANNERS

ACT ONE

SCENE ONE

The dining room. Saturday 6 p.m. A fine evening—sun streams through the large windows of the room. A solid table and four chairs. A sideboard. A window seat and a couple of additional upright chairs. The room is large and high ceilinged and like the rest of this Victorian vicarage-type building, badly needs redecorating.

ANNIE in baggy sweater, jeans and raffia slippers enters with a flower vase of water. She thumps this down in the middle of the table, picks up the roses which lie beside it and drops them into the vase. She gives the whole lot a final shake and that, as far as she's concerned, concludes her flower arrangement. She is moving to the sideboard, about to lay the table when SARAH enters. She wears a light summer coat and dress. She is breathless.

SARAH: Hallo! We're here—

ANNIE: Sarah!

SARAH: [*embracing her*] Annie dear. . .

ANNIE: Good journey?

SARAH: Oh yes, yes, not too bad. Reg drove far too fast as usual but we got here—oh, it's lovely to come down. I've been looking forward to this weekend away from it all for weeks. Weekend? It's barely a day. You've no idea how that dreary little house of ours gets me down.

ANNIE: Oh, it's not bad.

SARAH: Try living there sometime. Not a decent shop, not a cinema, not even a hairdresser—except some awful place I can't go into because of the smell. I said to Reg, for goodness sake you're an estate agent, surely you can get the pick of anywhere and then we finish up in somewhere like this . . . You're so lucky, Annie, you have no idea. Just to see a tree once in a while and the birds . . . I really miss it. Now then, how are you, let's look. Oh, Annie darling, you look just the same. Your hair . . .

ANNIE: [*self-consciously smoothing her tangle*] I know . . . I haven't brushed it today. I washed it, though, this morning.

SARAH: What's the good of washing it if you don't brush it. It's like a gorse bush.

ANNIE: Well, nobody sees it. The postman, the milkman, couple of cows and Mother.

SARAH: And Tom.

ANNIE: Oh, yes. Tom.

SARAH: You mustn't forget Tom. And how's Mother?

ANNIE: No better, no worse. She hasn't felt like getting up, not for weeks . . .

SARAH: Well, you should make her. She needs to.

ANNIE: Old Wickham says if she doesn't want to, don't make her.

SARAH: Wickham? Oh yes, I've never really cared for him. His eyes are too close together. Still, I suppose he's all right as a doctor. He must be better than ours. I mean, this business with my back was practically criminal.

ANNIE: Your back?

SARAH: Surely I wrote and told you? I'm sure I did. I was so upset I wrote to everybody.

ANNIE: Oh yes.

SARAH: Annie, I must buy you a new jumper, remind me.

ANNIE: I'm attached to this one.

SARAH: I should think you are . . . you were wearing it at Christmas. We'll have to chisel it off you . . . mmm, lovely flowers . . . Now tell me. Where are you going?

ANNIE: When?

SARAH: For your weekend, where are you going?

ANNIE: Well—

SARAH: Oh, come on. Don't be so secretive.

ANNIE: Well . . . I was going to Hastings.

SARAH: Oh, lovely! Hastings is gorgeous. I think I was there with Reg just before we were married. There's a heavenly little pub somewhere . . .

ANNIE: No, well I couldn't get in at Hastings.

SARAH: Couldn't get in?

ANNIE: No, it was all booked. I forgot it was summer.

SARAH: Oh. Yes. Well, where are you going?

ANNIE: I rather fancied East Grinstead.

SARAH: East Grinstead?

ANNIE: Yes.

SARAH: What an extraordinary idea. What on earth made you choose there?

ANNIE: Well, it sounded—interesting.

SARAH: Yes, I suppose it is. I've never heard of anybody having a holiday in East Grinstead. I suppose they do—but I've never heard of anybody.

ANNIE: Well, I am.

SARAH: Yes. I think I'd have almost preferred Eastbourne but . . . [*Displaying her outfit*] Do you like this?

ANNIE: Super.

SARAH: It was like a tent on me when I bought it, but I had it altered. I'm rather pleased. Now, you're to leave everything to me. I'm taking over. Just tell me what pills and potions Mother has and when she has them and then off you go.

ANNIE: I've written it down somewhere. I'll show you. The only difficult things are her drops.

SARAH: Oh well, if they're difficult Reg can cope with them. He's going to do most of the running up and down stairs anyway. I mean, this is a holiday for me too. She's his mother. He can do something for her for a change.

ANNIE: How is he?

SARAH: Reg? [*Big sigh*] Oh well, he's still Reg you know. I've tried. God knows I've tried but he'll always be basically Reg. You'll know, he's your brother after all. There are times when I think he's sleep walking. I have to force him to make an effort. Heaven knows how he runs a business. I'd certainly never let him sell a house of mine.

ANNIE: I've left you a cold supper.

SARAH: Oy, you shouldn't have bothered.

ANNIE: Well, I knew you wouldn't want to be . . .

SARAH: You shouldn't have bothered.

ANNIE: I left it all out for you on the—

SARAH: You really shouldn't have bothered.

ANNIE: —kitchen table.

SARAH: Lovely.

ANNIE: I was just laying things in here.

SARAH: Oh, there's no need for that. We'll eat with our fingers. We're on holiday, for heaven's sake.

ANNIE: We do have knives and forks.

SARAH: I'll find them, don't bother. Now please, just get changed and go.

ANNIE: Okay. [*She starts to move to the door.*]

SARAH: Oh. I nearly forgot. How's Tom?

ANNIE: Tom? Oh, fine. I think.

SARAH: Still seeing a lot of him?

ANNIE: Oh, yes. He's generally around. When he's not out curing his sick animals. He's here at the moment, actually. The cat's got something wrong with its paw.

SARAH: It must be fascinating being a vet. It's a pity in a way he's not a proper doctor.

ANNIE: He is a proper doctor. He just prefers animals to people.

SARAH: That came from the heart.

ANNIE: No. He just likes animals. Don't think he's very fond of our cat but he likes most animals.

SARAH: Yes, he's a bit—heavy going, isn't he? I've always found him a trifle ponderous. Perhaps it's shyness.

ANNIE: No, I think he's probably ponderous.

SARAH: He hasn't—er—shown any more interest?

ANNIE: In what?

SARAH: Well, you. At Christmas, we thought he was beginning to sit up and take notice of you just a little. Pricking up his ears.

ANNIE: Like a mongrel with a pedigree bitch.

SARAH: Yes, well . . .

ANNIE: Honestly, stop trying to pair us off. He just comes round when he's bored, that's all.

SARAH: A man doesn't spend as much time as Tom does round here without having a very good reason. Believe you me. You don't have to be psychic to know what that is.

ANNIE: Well, if it's that he's never asked for it and even if he did he wouldn't get it. So I don't know why he bothers.

SARAH: Annie! You're getting dreadfully coarse.

ANNIE: Oh, you're just a prude.

SARAH: No, I'm not a prude. No, I've never been called that. You can't call me a prude. That's not fair, Annie, I mean, I don't care for smutty talk or dirty jokes. I just don't find them funny. Or particularly tasteful. But that isn't being a prude. That's normal decent behaviour which is something quite different.

ANNIE: Yes.

SARAH: I won't have the television set on at all these days.

ANNIE: Anyway, all that happens is that Tom comes round here like he has done for years. I feed him. He sits and broods. Sometimes we talk. That's all.

SARAH: Talk about what?

ANNIE: Oh, super exciting things like does the kitchen ceiling need another coat and distemper and hardpad and foot and mouth and swine vesicular disease. Then I pot Mother and retire to bed—alone—itching.

SARAH: Oh.

ANNIE: And count sick sheep crashing headlong into the gate. Look for all I know he may be passionately in love with me. He may be flashing out all sorts of secret signals which I just haven't noticed. But he's never even put a hand on my knee. [*Reflecting*] God forbid.

SARAH: But you're fond of him?

ANNIE: He's—very kind. Yes, I like him a lot. I sometimes miss him when he's not here. I suppose that means something.

SARAH: Yes. You see, I was rather hoping—I know it's wicked of me—I was rather hoping that you were both planning to go off for this weekend together.

ANNIE: Oh. No.

SARAH: You're not, are you?

ANNIE: [*uneasy*] No. Not at all.

SARAH: Are you sure?

ANNIE: Of course I'm sure.

SARAH: You're looking very shifty.

ANNIE: I'm not. Honestly. No. Stop it.

SARAH: Stop what?

ANNIE: Looking at me like that.

SARAH: Like what?

ANNIE: Like that. Stop it.

SARAH: You're a dreadful liar.

ANNIE: I'm not.

SARAH: Listen, if you are, there's no need to keep it a secret from me. I mean, you said I'm a prude but I've just proved I'm not, surely? I mentioned it first. I think it's splendid. I think if you and Tom were to get away from this house, away from Mother and everything—it's the best thing you could do. It's what you both need. [*She kisses her.*] Very sensible.

ANNIE: Yes.

SARAH: Have a lovely time. I only wish it were me. Not with Tom, of course. But I think that's what we all need now and then, don't we? A nice dirty weekend somewhere. Oh, it's so exciting. I am pleased you're doing it. I think the best bit is waking up in the morning in a strange room and finding some exciting looking man beside you and—you've got a double room?

ANNIE: It's a bit more complicated than that.

SARAH: Oh? How do you mean? You haven't got a double room.

ANNIE: No, it's just . . .

SARAH: What? You're not pregnant?

ANNIE: No.

SARAH: Oh, thank God.

ANNIE: No, it's just—oh golly, I didn't mean to tell you.

SARAH: Tell me what?

ANNIE: It's awfully sordid. You're sure you want to hear?

SARAH: Of course, I want to hear.

ANNIE: It'll shock you.

SARAH: My dear, I've been married for eight years. I've had two children. I think I've just about seen everything there is to see. I defy you to shock me. I honestly defy you.

ANNIE: Well. Last Christmas, when you were all here . . .

SARAH: Yes?

ANNIE: You and Reg and Ruth and Norman. And then you and Reg left early . . .

SARAH: Because Denise didn't want to miss her dancing classes—yes?

ANNIE: And then after that, Ruth was ill . . .

SARAH: Or so she said.

ANNIE: Well, she was flat on her back with something for a week and that left Norman and me—more or less to cope. Tom was in Scotland on a course.

SARAH: Yes?

ANNIE: Anyway.

SARAH: I'm beginning dreadfully not to like the sound of this one little bit.

ANNIE: Anyway. Golly, I'm getting dreadfully hot.

SARAH: Go on. What?

ANNIE: Well, you know Norman, he's . . .

SARAH: Yes, I know Norman very well.

ANNIE: He's not a bit like Tom. I mean, just the opposite to Tom. Norman doesn't bother with secret signals at all. It was just wham, thump and there we both were on the rug.

SARAH: Rug?

ANNIE: Yes.

SARAH: Which rug?

ANNIE: The brown nylon fur one in the lounge . . .[*She starts to giggle.*]

SARAH: [*irritated*] What is it? Why are you laughing?

ANNIE: [*unable to control herself*] Does it matter which rug?

SARAH: I don't think it's funny.

ANNIE: No, nor do I. I'm sorry—it's just I'm so embarrassed—oh, gosh—

SARAH: Annie, pull yourself together.

ANNIE: [*is helpless*] Yes . . .

SARAH: [*thumping the table*] Annie, what happened on the rug?

ANNIE: Everything happened on the rug.

SARAH: Does Ruth know?

ANNIE: No.

SARAH: Or Tom?

ANNIE: No. [*Drying her eyes*] Oh dear . . .

SARAH: Well, I blame Norman. That is absolutely typical . . . fur rug! [*This starts* ANNIE *off again.*] It's just the sort of thing—Annie, will you stop making that ridiculous noise . . . typical behaviour. [ANNIE *blows her nose.*] Is that it? Was that the only occasion?

ANNIE: Oh yes. Ruth got better and they both went home.

SARAH: I suppose it could have been worse. That poor woman. I mean, I don't have a lot of time for Ruth, as you know. Personally, I find her snide little remarks, her violent ups and downs just too much to cope with. I know she's your sister, I'm sorry for talking like this. However, I would not wish my worst enemy married to a man like . . . not even Ruth. Heaven knows why they married. Never understood it. What did she see in him?

ANNIE: Norman says it was uncontrollable animal lust that drew them together.

SARAH: Norman told you that?

ANNIE: Yes. He says it's died out now. They are like two empty husks.

SARAH: Yes. Hardly surprising. Well, believe me, you're well clear of that, dear. You're well clear of that one.

ANNIE: You don't think I should then?

SARAH: What?

ANNIE: Go.

SARAH: Go where?

ANNIE: This weekend.

SARAH: This weekend?

ANNIE: With Norman? To East Grinstead.

[*A pause.*]

SARAH: You were planning to go with Norman to East Grinstead?

ANNIE: Yes. He couldn't get in anywhere else.

SARAH: You're not serious?

ANNIE: Yes.

SARAH: But how could you even think of it?

ANNIE: He asked me.

SARAH: What has that to do with it?

ANNIE: Well, I wanted a holiday . . .

SARAH: Yes but—this wouldn't be just a holiday . . . I mean, I mean, you just don't go off on holiday with your sister's husband.

ANNIE: It was only a weekend. I needed a holiday.

SARAH: Well, you could have gone on your own.

ANNIE: [*slightly angry*] I didn't want to go on my own. I'm always on my own.

SARAH: But did you realize what you would be getting yourself into?

ANNIE: Well—the way Norman put it—it sounded simple. Just a weekend.

SARAH: Norman will put it any way which suits Norman. Did you think of Ruth? And Tom?

ANNIE: Oh, to hell with Tom. He could have asked me if he'd wanted to but he didn't. If I wait to be asked by Tom, I won't even get on an old folks' outing.

SARAH: Well, what about Ruth?

ANNIE: That's up to Norman. He wrote to me and then he phoned and asked me and I suddenly thought, well yes . . . I think actually if I'm being really truthful and, knowing Norman, I didn't think it would ever happen.

SARAH: You were certain enough about it to get Reg and

I down. We've had all the trouble of having to take the children to their grandparents so that we wouldn't have to bring them down here because we knew they would disturb Mother. I've had all the trouble of delegating responsibility for the "Bring and Buy Sale" which I'm sure will be a disaster because I'm the only one among them with any sort of organizing ability. And Reg has had to cancel his golf.

ANNIE: I'm sorry. I've been feeling sick all morning. I'm sorry.

SARAH: Yes, well I'm sure we all are.

ANNIE: Well . . . [*She moves to the door.*]

SARAH: Where are you going?

ANNIE: I don't know. I was just—I don't know.

SARAH: I think it's just as well we are here. You quite obviously need a rest. Now, I want you to sit down here and leave everything to me.

ANNIE: No, it's all right I—

SARAH: And let's get this quite clear to start with. You are not going anywhere. Not while I'm in this house.

ANNIE: What about my weekend?

SARAH: You can have your weekend here. Reg and I will cope. That's what we came down for. You can rest. You can certainly forget the idea of going anywhere with Norman. That's final. You're staying here.

ANNIE: Yes, I rather thought I would be.

SARAH: What you need is rest.

[TOM *enters.*]

TOM: Ah.

SARAH: Tom! How nice to see you, Tom.

TOM: Hallo, Sarah. Keeping fit?

SARAH: Tom, I've just been saying I think Annie's honestly been overdoing it.

TOM: Really? Do you think so?

SARAH: You really must take more care of her, Tom. We all expect you to keep an eye on her, you know, when we're not here.

TOM: Do my best.

SARAH: She's rather your responsibility.

TOM: Yes, can't have that. Been trying to get that cat out of the tree. Your cat's gone up a tree, Annie.

ANNIE: Oh.

SARAH: Anyway, Annie's just decided she's not going away this weekend. She's going to stay here and have a good rest.

TOM: Septic paw, you know.

SARAH: And Reg and I will be here to look after her.

TOM: That's good news. Aren't you going then?

ANNIE: No.

SARAH: With your help of course, Tom. You must stay for supper.

TOM: Supper?

SARAH: Mustn't he, Annie?

ANNIE: Why not.

TOM: Save me opening a tin at home.

SARAH: Lovely. Now, I must just pop up and see Mother. Then I'll come down and organize everything. Leave it all to Reg and me. Where is Reg? I asked him to bring the cases in ages ago.

TOM: I left him in the garden.

SARAH: What's he doing in the garden?

TOM: Nothing much. Just talking to Norman.

SARAH: Norman? Norman is here?

TOM: Yes.

SARAH: Norman is here, under this roof?

TOM: No, he's in the garden. We were chatting away.

SARAH: Oh, my God. Chatting about what?

TOM: Various subjects. Cats. And his pyjamas.

SARAH: Pyjamas?

TOM: Yes, he was showing them to me.

SARAH: Do you mean he's wearing them?

TOM: No. He was just generally waving them about.

SARAH: Tom, stay here with Annie. Don't move. Stay here. I'll be back.

[SARAH *hurries out*.]

TOM: Did you know Norman was here?

ANNIE: Yes. I saw him earlier.

TOM: Oh. Were you expecting him?

ANNIE: Not really, no.

TOM: Ah. Well. [*He stares out of the window.*]

ANNIE: [*in frustration*] Oh.

TOM: Put your feet up.

ANNIE: What?

TOM: I should put your feet up.

ANNIE: [*rising and going to the sideboard*] No. Not at the moment.

TOM: I'm a bit worried about that paw, you know.

ANNIE: [*taking out cutlery*] Paw?

TOM: On the cat. Needs looking at. Does he have a name, by the way?

ANNIE: What? No. Just cat.

TOM: That's all right, I don't suppose he minds. Preferable to Oscar or Herbert or something. He probably wouldn't answer to it if he had one. Cats' names are more for human benefit. They give one a certain degree more confidence that the animal belongs to you. Of course, they never do. Cats belong to no-one but themselves.

ANNIE: Oh, I'm so stupid . . . [*She bangs down the cutlery.*]

TOM: All right?

ANNIE: Yes. I just feel such a fool.

TOM: Oh. Not much answer to that, is there? [*Finding a round tin biscuit barrel in the sideboard and opening it*] Mind if I have a water biscuit?

ANNIE: Have the lot.

TOM: No. Just one. It'll spoil my dinner. Ah, high baked . . .

ANNIE: Tom . . .

TOM: [*crunching*] Um?

ANNIE: What did you think when I said I was going away this weekend?

TOM: Well, I don't know. I suppose I thought—you were going away this weekend. (*Holding out the tin*) Want one?

ANNIE: [*irritated*] No . . .

TOM: They're a bit stale. No, it did occur to me you might have liked someone to come along with you . . .

ANNIE: It did?

TOM: And then I thought, well, probably not.

ANNIE: Why? What on earth made you think I wanted to go off and sit in some dreary hotel room on my own?

TOM: Yes, it did seem rather odd, I must say.

ANNIE: How long have you known me?

TOM: Oh—years . . .

ANNIE: Years. And in all that time have I ever even hinted that I'd like to go off on my own?

TOM: Not as far as I know.

ANNIE: [*angrily*] Then why the hell should I suddenly decide to do it now?

TOM: Well, I don't know. Simmer down.

ANNIE: Why didn't you say—Annie, will you be all right on your own? Would you like company? Someone to come along too? Someone to talk to? Why didn't you think of saying it? Just once.

TOM: Oh, come on . . .

ANNIE: Or was the whole prospect just too awful?

TOM: No—

ANNIE: Well, then?

TOM: You should have said something. You should have asked me along. I'd've come. You should've asked me.

ANNIE: [*weakly*] Oh, dear God. Yes, I'd have had to have done.

TOM: Don't blame me.

ANNIE: I'm not blaming you. Oh—nun's knickers!

TOM: Language. You're getting awfully het up. I should put your feet up.

ANNIE: I don't want to put my bloody feet up.

[ANNIE *stamps out.* TOM *gazes after her, slightly puzzled. He helps himself to another biscuit. After a second,* REG *bursts in.*]

REG: Where is she then? Where's that little sister of mine? [*Seeing no-one but* TOM] Oh. Where is she?

TOM: No idea. Kitchen, possibly.

REG: Ah. He's a laugh, you know.

TOM: Who?

REG: Norman. Goes on and on. Don't know what he's talking about. Makes me laugh though. I don't care, I like him. She doesn't but I do. Women don't, you know. Not many women like him. Don't know why. Sarah can't bear him. Won't have him in the house. Nor will his wife. [*He laughs.*]

TOM: I think Annie gets on all right with him.

REG: Ah well. Annie. [*He smiles affectionately.*] She's something special. You'll be all right with her, Tom. Take my word. If you decide to marry any of us, marry her. Not that I'm saying you should but if you did. Mind you, you can't marry Ruth and I don't think you'd fancy me so there's not much choice, is there? [*He laughs.*]

TOM: Um. [*Thoughtfully*] They're all a bit peculiar at the moment.

REG: Who are?

TOM: The women. All on edge, for some reason.

REG: The women are restless tonight, eh? Full moon.

TOM: Eh?

REG: Probably a full moon. [*He bays like a hound and laughs.*]

TOM: No. Something startled them.

REG: Norman. Or mice. One or the other. I hear Annie's not going now.

TOM: Apparently not.

REG: Could have had my golf. If I'd known. Never mind. Better go and see Mother in a minute. Sarah's up there at the moment. I'll wait till she comes down. Two of them, too much of a good thing. I'll put it off as long as I can. Mother always says the same thing. What did you go and marry her for? Biggest mistake of your life. You'll live to regret it. Trouble is, I can never think of a convincing answer. [*He laughs.*] She's probably right. I mean, there are compensations. Children—sometimes. Even Sarah—

sometimes. But when I sit here in this house and listen to the quiet. You know, I wonder why I left. I had my own room here, you know. All my books, my own desk, a shelf for my hobbies. I'd sit up there in my school holidays . . . happy as a sandboy. I'd make these balsa wood aeroplanes. Dozens of them. Very satisfying. Mind you, they never flew. Soon as I launched them—crack—nose dive —firewood. But it didn't really matter. It was a hell of a bore winding them up, anyway. I built one for the kids the other day. They didn't really take to it. Where's the guns, Dad? Where are the bombs then? [*He shakes his head.*] Oh well, what do you expect.

TOM: No, you see—I think I've stopped her from going.

REG: Who?

TOM: Annie.

REG: You have?

TOM: Yes . . .

REG: Hope we'll get some dinner soon. I'm getting peckish.

TOM: You see, she didn't want to go on her own.

REG: On holiday? Ah, well. Who does? [*He finds the biscuits.*]

TOM: She was rather expecting me to offer to come too.

REG: Oh. You should have been in there—like a shot, eh?

TOM: Yes.

REG: I would have been, in your shoes. These are stale.

TOM: Now I've gone and upset her.

REG: Oh dear.

TOM: I've never been very good at that sort of thing. Always seem to miss the moment.

REG: That's how it goes, isn't it?

TOM: Yes. I've let her down. I suppose I'll have to find a way of making it up.

REG: I shouldn't bother. It'll blow over. Wait for the new moon.

[SARAH *enters.*]

SARAH: What are you doing in here?

REG: Oh. I beg your pardon. Is the dining room closed? [*He laughs to* TOM.]

SARAH: Where's Annie?

REG: Getting us something to eat, I hope. Slaving over a hot stove.

SARAH: She is not. Anyway, it's a cold meal. Where is she?

REG: I don't know.

SARAH: You haven't left her in the living room with Norman?

REG: Possibly. What's wrong? He's all right, he won't bite her.

SARAH: Oh, my God.

REG: Tom'll inject her for rabies, won't you, Tom?

TOM: I'll go and look for her if you . . .

REG: Inject her for rabies.

SARAH: No, Tom, stay where you are. Reg.

REG: What?

SARAH: Go and see if they're in there.

REG: Why don't you?

SARAH: Because I'd rather you did, please.

REG: I'm not interested if they're in there. It doesn't matter to me if they're in there or not. You're the one who's interested if they're in there.

SARAH: [*sharply*] Will you please do as I ask for once? Besides it'll look much more natural.

TOM: I say, what's going on?

SARAH: [*soothingly*] Nothing to worry about, Tom, nothing at all.

REG: I don't think it'll look more natural. I mean, what's natural about me walking in there, having a look and then walking out again?

SARAH: Well, pretend you've gone to fetch something. Use your imagination, for heaven's sake.

REG: All right. All right. What am I suppose to be fetching?

SARAH: I don't know. Anything.

REG: [*moving to the door and then, pausing*] What's all this about a cold meal? What sort of cold meal?

SARAH: Cold meat and salad. Now, go on.

REG: If there's one thing I can't stand when I'm hungry it's salad.

[REG *goes out.*]

SARAH: He's a difficult man. He is such a difficult man. Ask him to do a simple thing for you and there's a twenty minute argument. Did you talk to Annie?

TOM: Yes.

SARAH: Did she—say anything?

TOM: She—told me the reason why she'd planned the whole weekend. Why it had fallen through.

SARAH: Oh.

TOM: I could kick myself for being so slow off the mark.

SARAH: You mustn't blame yourself.

TOM: I'm afraid I do, rather.

SARAH: I don't see why. I mean, you weren't to know that—

[REG *re-enters with a wastepaper basket.*]

REG: Yes, they're in there.

SARAH: What's that?

REG: Wastepaper basket, isn't it?

SARAH: Couldn't you have found something a little more natural?

REG: What did you expect me to bring back? A bloody grand piano?

SARAH: Right, Tom.

TOM: Um?

SARAH: I think it's high time you went in and said your piece.

TOM: Really?

SARAH: Told them where you stand.

TOM: Me?

SARAH: Make sure Norman knows.

TOM: Norman?

SARAH: You'll lose your chance if you don't do it soon.

TOM: [*baffled*] Oh yes.

[REG *bays like a hound.*]

SARAH: What are you doing?

REG: Nothing. Full moon, that's all. Full moon. [*He nods and winks at* TOM.]

TOM: Ah.

[TOM *goes out bewildered.*]

SARAH: I think this may have worked out for the best. Might even stir Tom into action, you never know. You haven't been eating these biscuits?

REG: I squelched through a couple.

SARAH: You'll spoil your meal.

REG: Oh yes. All that lovely lettuce.

SARAH: You and your stomach. I'd rather hoped I was in for a quiet weekend for once. It seems it's not to be. Look at these forks, they haven't been cleaned since we were last here . . . It's a crying shame. All this silver.

REG: Are we staying or going?

SARAH: We can hardly go home.

REG: I thought the whole point of our being here was to look after Mother but if Annie's going to be here . . .

SARAH: I don't know about being here to look after Mother. We need someone here to look after her.

REG: She's managed up till now. There's Tom.

SARAH: Oh, Tom. There's no point in relying on him. I mean, he's pleasant enough but I don't think he's quite all there. That's a terrible thing to say but look at the way he's behaved. Mind you, she does precious little to encourage him. How is she going to attract any man looking like that, let alone Tom?

REG: She's all right. Leave her alone.

SARAH: Do you realize what would happen if I did?

REG: She can manage.

SARAH: I take it you've gathered what's going on in this house?

REG: What?

SARAH: Where have you been for the last hour?

REG: What do you mean, where have I been? You know where I've been. I've been here, waiting for something to eat.

SARAH: Norman had planned to take Annie away to a hotel this weekend.

REG: Norman?

SARAH: Yes.

REG: With Annie?

SARAH: Yes.

REG: Was she the one he was taking to East Grinstead?

SARAH: [*impatiently*] Of course she was.

[REG *gives a yell of delight.*]

SARAH: [*when this has died down, coolly*] Frankly, Reg, I think there's something mentally wrong with you. I think you ought to see someone. I'm being serious. How can you take so little interest in your own family, your own sister.

REG: Oh, Sarah, come on. Sit down. You've done nothing but run round and round . . . I think it's funny, I can't help it.

SARAH: You're the same at home. Exactly the same.

REG: Oh, now, come on . . . [*He moves away.*]

SARAH: Yes, you can walk away but it's always left for me to deal with, isn't it? It's left for me to apologize to people for you. It's left to me to explain why you walk straight upstairs as soon as anyone comes to visit us.

REG: They're your friends.

SARAH: It's me that's left looking stupid in front of the headmistress when you forget the names of our own children—

REG: That was only once.

SARAH: They run wild those children. You've done nothing for them. Nothing at all. If I didn't get them food, they'd starve, if I didn't buy them clothes, they'd be naked— you sit in that room, which I spend my whole life trying to keep tidy, fiddling with aeroplanes and bits of cardboard and now you can't even be bothered with your own sister—

REG: Sarah please, would you kindly stop talking.

SARAH: No, I will not stop talking.

REG: You have talked at me since I got up this morning—
you have talked at me over breakfast—

SARAH: It happens to be the only way I can get through to
you—

REG: You talked solidly in the car for an hour—nearly
causing us to have a very serious accident . . .

SARAH: Which was entirely your fault.

REG: And ever since we've been here, you haven't stopped
for a second. Now, for the love of God, shut up.
[*Slight pause.*]

SARAH: I will not be spoken to like that. [*Tearful now*] I
will not have you raising your voice to me like that. Just
who do you think it is you're talking to?

REG: I think, like you, I'm talking to a brick wall. I'm going
for a walk.

SARAH: [*hysterically*] All right, go. Go on then. Go, you
beastly little man.
[SARAH *snatches up the biscuit tin from the table and hurls it at*
REG. *It hits the sideboard, biscuits fly in all directions.*]

REG: Sarah!
[SARAH *sits sobbing.* REG *stands uselessly.* ANNIE *comes in.*]

ANNIE: Oh.
[REG *starts to pick up the biscuits.*]

REG: Biscuits.

ANNIE: [*moving to him*] Oh yes. Here, let me . . . [*Mouthing
to* REG] What's the matter?

REG: [*mouthing*] Nothing.

ANNIE: [*pointing at* SARAH, *mouthing*] Is she all right?
[REG *shrugs.*]
[*looking at him and shrugging*] I'll get the dustpan.
[ANNIE *goes out.*]

SARAH: You're contemptible.

REG: You really must control that temper of yours, you
know.
[TOM *enters. He pauses as he takes in the scene.* REG, *crawling
on the floor, does not see him. Nor does* SARAH *with her back to
him.*

SARAH: You are the most contemptible man I've ever known.

REG: The feeling's mutual, don't worry.

[TOM *goes out looking worried.*]

SARAH: God knows what's going to happen to us. God knows.

[ANNIE *returns with the dustpan.*]

ANNIE: Here we are. Soon clear this up.

REG: Sorry about this.

ANNIE: Oh well. Accidents happen, don't they?

SARAH: It wasn't an accident.

ANNIE: Oh.

REG: No. The biscuits were so stale they threw themselves off the table in desperation.

SARAH: What have you decided, Annie?

ANNIE: What? Oh well—it's all rather settled itself, hasn't it? I'm staying here of course.

SARAH: I mean, it's entirely up to you. I mean, all I was doing was trying to—

ANNIE: Well, it's probably best.

SARAH: Tom and Norman have sorted out their differences have they?

ANNIE: I don't think there were any really. Norman's getting drunk and Tom's looking thoughtful.

SARAH: Oh well, I've done what I can. I'm sorry, I think the man must be mentally defective. I think they both are. I'll bring some things in.

ANNIE: It's all right, I'll—

SARAH: No—no—no! I want to. I want to bring some things in.

[SARAH *goes out.*]

REG: We seem to have upset your weekend.

ANNIE: Not really. It was a mad idea. Rather flattering all the same. Suddenly having two men bidding for my favours. Even if they are Tom and Norman.

REG: [*chuckling*] Well, I must say . . . didn't know I had a sister like you.

ANNIE: [*amused*] It's ridiculous really.

REG: I knew one of us took after Mother—I couldn't think who it was. Certainly it wasn't me or Ruth.

ANNIE: Not Ruth.

REG: Do you remember Mother taking us on holiday? Where was it? Weston-super-Mare. Were you old enough to remember?

ANNIE: You mean during the war? When she picked up that sailor?

REG: Yes. He kept throwing that ball half a mile down the beach. Trying to get us all to run after it. Run along, kids. Go and fetch it. Let me talk to your Mum.

ANNIE: And Ruth wouldn't go.

REG: No, she wouldn't budge.

ANNIE: "I'm staying here to look after Mother. I don't trust him . . ." There was Mother saying, "Run along, Ruth dear. Run along and play . . ."

REG: Then there was that Polish rear-gunner.

ANNIE: Oh God, yes. And Father suddenly came home on leave.

REG: That drainpipe's still broken you know. I had a look. [*They laugh.* SARAH *enters, carrying a tray of plates. She bangs this down and glares at them.* ANNIE *and* REG *are silent.*]

SARAH: [*icily*] Don't let me spoil the joke. I'm sure you both find me terribly amusing. I'm sure you all find me hilarious.

ANNIE: Not at all.

[TOM *comes on laughing heartily.* SARAH *wheels on him and glares.* TOM *stops laughing.* SARAH *goes out.*]
Sarah . . .
[ANNIE *goes out after* SARAH.]

REG: What was the joke?

TOM: Nothing really. Norman told me to come in and try to jolly things up. Doesn't seem to have worked.

REG: Hardly at all.

[NORMAN *is heard singing briefly from the sitting room.* REG *and* TOM *register.*]

TOM: [*holding up a bottle*] I brought a bottle of this. Help wash down the radishes. Managed to salvage it. Norman's drunk most of them.

REG: I didn't know we had anything like that in this house.

TOM: Home-made. Mother made it last year. Just before she was ill. Annie and I bottled it. Tastes revolting but it's very potent.

REG: Carrot. Does it have to be carrot?

TOM: [*opening the bottle*] Well, there's also parsnip or dandelion but this seems to have a slightly better bouquet. The dandelion's all right but I lost the use of one side of my face for about an hour after I drunk it. [*Handing a glass to* REG] Here, what do you think?

REG: [*tasting it*] Not bad. Not bad at all. [*As it hits his stomach*] Oh, good grief.

TOM: I think it's an acquired taste. Cheers.

REG: You must have a stomach like a blast furnace.
  [*Another brief burst of song from* NORMAN *then* ANNIE *and* SARAH *return with the rest of the first course.*]

ANNIE: Grub's up.

REG: Ah-ha, the great caterpillar hunt is on.

ANNIE: No it isn't, I washed the lettuce this time.

REG: Oh yes.

ANNIE: Well, I rinsed it under the tap. Twice.

TOM: Shall I give Norman a call?

SARAH: No.

REG: What I always say about your salads, Annie, is that I may not enjoy eating them but I learn an awful lot about insect biology. My appreciation of the anatomy of an earwig has increased enormously . . .

SARAH: Could we keep off this subject, please.

TOM: Wine, Sarah?

SARAH: What is it?

TOM: Wine. Home-made.

SARAH: Oh well, just a little. Thank you.
  [TOM *pours* ANNIE *a glass. They sit and eat in silence.*]

REG: Could you pass the centipede sauce please.

[ANNIE *giggles*. SARAH *glares*.]

[*raising his glass*] Well, here's to us.

SARAH: I think it would be fitting to drink to Annie and Tom.

TOM: Really? Why is that?

ANNIE: Because we're here.

TOM: Oh, I see. I thought there was a special reason.

SARAH: That's rather up to you, isn't it, Tom?

TOM: Um?

REG: Cheers, anyway.

SARAH: Good health, Tom, Annie.

[SARAH *drinks, puts down her glass. Her stomach explodes. She lets out a gasp.* TOM *and* ANNIE *half rise.*]

ANNIE: Sarah!

TOM: All right? [*He begins to bang her back rather heartily.*]

SARAH: [*regaining her breath*] Yes—it took me by surprise.

ANNIE: Yes, it tends to do that.

SARAH: [*not enjoying* TOM's *attentions*] That will do, Tom, thank you. That will do.

REG: It'll kill off any beetles you've swallowed.

SARAH: Will you stop making remarks like that.

REG: [*raising his knife by way of apology*] Sorry . . . sorry.

SARAH: For goodness sake. For once in this family, let's try and have a civilized meal.

[*They eat in silence. From a distance* NORMAN *is heard singing in the living room. They hear this, catch each other's eyes and then, under* SARAH's *withering gaze, continue to eat. As* NORMAN's *singing becomes louder and more boisterous,* ANNIE, TOM *and* REG *become helpless with stifled laughter.*]

Curtain

ACT ONE

SCENE TWO

The dining room. Sunday morning, 9 a.m. NORMAN *is standing in his pyjamas and bare feet. He is whistling. After a moment,* SARAH, *fully dressed comes in with a tray of breakfast things.*

NORMAN: [*cheerfully*] Morning.
SARAH: [*seeing him*] Oh. [*She unloads the tray, ignoring him.*]
NORMAN: Lovely morning. Hear the birds?
    [SARAH *continues grimly with her task.*]
    Sleep well? Hope you slept well. I slept well.
    [SARAH *goes out.* NORMAN *starts to whistle again and examines what she has put on the table.* ANNIE *enters. She carries another tray of breakfast things.*]
    Morning.
ANNIE: [*seeing him*] Oh.
    [ANNIE *starts unloading her tray, ignoring him.*]
NORMAN: Lovely morning. Sleep well, did you? I slept like a log. Must have been that wine. Wonderful. It's a rotten drink but it makes a lovely sleeping draught. I'd market it. Sleep nature's way with our dandelion brew. Arhar . . .
    [ANNIE *goes out passing* SARAH *coming in with the last of the breakfast things.*]
NORMAN: What have we got for breakfast, then? What have we got?
SARAH: [*calling*] Reg? Breakfast.
REG: [*off, distant*] Right . . .
NORMAN: How's old Reg this morning? All right, is he? Sleep well, did he? . . . I can tell you I can do with some breakfast. Missed my meal last night. Did you know that? I missed my meal. I didn't hear the dinner gong. What sort of hotel do you call this?
    [ANNIE *returns.*]
SARAH: Have you taken Mother hers up?

ANNIE: Yes.

NORMAN: I'll sit here, shall I? All right if I sit here? Anybody any objections if I sit here? [*He is ignored.*] I'll sit here.

[NORMAN *sits at the head of the table.* SARAH *sits at the other end with* ANNIE *close to her, isolating* NORMAN. NORMAN *sits whistling.* REG *enters.*]

REG: [*cheerily*] Morning all.

NORMAN: Morning.

REG: [*his face falling*] Oh.

[REG *sits next to* SARAH. ANNIE *and* REG *have cereal.* SARAH *butters toast.*]

NORMAN: Well, you're a right cheery lot, aren't you? Look at you. A right cheery lot. Woo-hoo . . . hallooo . . . [*He waves at them.*]

SARAH: [*acid*] Nobody in this house is speaking to you ever again.

NORMAN: Oh, I see. I see. That's the way the Swiss rolls. I see. That's the way the apple crumbles, is it? Oh ho. That's the way the corn flakes . . . [*A pause. He ponders. Suddenly sharply*] Sarah! Be careful! The butter . . .

SARAH: [*alarmed*] What?

NORMAN: Ha-ha! You spoke to me. Caught you. Caught you. [*Pause.*] All right, I'll talk to myself then. [*Very rapidly, in two voices*] Hallo, Norman—good morning, Norman—how are you, Norman—I'm very well, Norman—that's good news, Norman—

ANNIE: Shut up, Norman.

NORMAN: Ha-ha! Caught you again. That's two of you. Just got to catch old Reg now. Two out of three. Just Reg left . . . [*slight pause*] Look out, Reg! [*No reaction.*] Ah—can't catch him that way. [*Sharply*] Hey, Reg! . . . oh well. If that's the way it is. Don't talk to me. I don't care. Doesn't bother me. I don't know why you're all being so unsociable. All right, I had a few drinks last night. What's wrong with that? Hasn't anyone round this table ever had a drink then? Come on, I don't believe

it. You've had a drink haven't you, Reg? Ha-ha! Ha-ha!
Caught you. You spoke.

REG: No, I didn't.

NORMAN: Ha-ha! Three to me. I've won. [*Pause*] Nothing
wrong in a few drinks. Don't speak. I don't care. Going
to be a pretty dull Sunday if we all sit in silence, I can tell
you. Well, I'm not sitting in silence. I'll find something
to do. I know, I'll go up and frighten Mother.

[SARAH *looks up sharply and gives him a terrible glare.*]

Ah-ha! Nearly got you again. Is it too much to ask for
something to eat?

[*No response.*]

It's too much to ask for something to eat.

[*He gets up and moves down the table and takes the cereal bowl
that* SARAH *isn't using.*]

May I borrow your bowl? That's awfully nice of you.
And your spoon? Thank you. Now then, what shall I
have? [*Examining cereal packets*] Puffa Puffa rice. Ah-ha . . .

[*He returns to the top of the table, sits and fills his bowl.*]

No Sunday papers. Dear, dear. Ah, well I shall have to
read my morning cereal . . . [*He laughs*] Cereal. Do we all
get that? Apparently we don't. [*He reads. Suddenly, violently
banging the table*] Stop!

[*The others jump involuntarily.*]

Stop everything. Listen. A free pair of pinking shears for
only 79p and six Puffa Puffa tokens. Hurry, hurry, hurry.
What's this? Is nobody hurrying? Do you mean to tell me
that none of you want them? Where's the spirit of British
pinking? Dead, presumably. Like my relations. [*He eats a
handful of dry cereal thoughtfully*] Hang on, I've got another
game. Mind reading. I'll read your minds. Now then,
where shall we start? Sarah. Sarah is thinking—that noisy
man up there should be home with his wife. What is he
doing shattering the calm of our peaceful Sunday breakfast with his offers of reduced price pinking shears? Why
is he here, shouting at us like this? Why isn't he at home,
like any other decent husband, shouting at his wife? He

came down here to seduce his wife's own sister. How low can he get? The fact that his wife's own sister said, at one stage anyway, that she was perfectly happy to go along with him is beside the point. The fact that little Annie here was perfectly happy to ditch old reliable Tom— without a second thought—and come off with me is beside the point. We won't mention that because it doesn't quite fit in with the facts as we would like them. And what is little Annie thinking, I wonder? Maybe furtively admiring my pyjamas, who knows? Pyjamas that could have been hers. With all that they contain. These nearly were mine. Or maybe she is thinking . . . Phew, that was a close shave. I could have been shacked up in some dreadful hotel with this man—at this very moment . . . what a lucky escape for me. Thank heavens, I am back here at home amidst my talkative family exchanging witty breakfast banter. Knowing my two-legged faithful companion and friend, Tom the rambling vet, is even now planning to propose to me in 1997 just as soon as he's cured our cat. Meanwhile, I can live here peacefully, totally fulfilled, racing up and down stairs looking after Mother, having the time of my life and living happily ever after until I'm fifty-five and fat . . . I'm glad I didn't go to that hotel. Well, let me tell you so am I. I wouldn't want a weekend with you, anyway. And I'll tell you the funniest thing of all, shall I? . . .

[ANNIE *gets up and runs out.*]

[*Yelling furiously after her*] I didn't even book the hotel. I knew you wouldn't come. You didn't have the guts.

[*A pause.*]

SARAH: You can be very cruel, can't you Norman?

[SARAH *goes out after* ANNIE.]

NORMAN: Oh, well. It's a bit quieter without those two. Hear yourself speak. Too damned noisy before. All that crunching of toast. Like a brigade of Guards marching on gravel. Well now, Reg—

[REG *chews glumly through his cereal.*]

[*Looking round the table*] Milk? Ah. [*He gets up.*] Sugar? [*He returns with these and sits. Pouring milk over his cereal*] Nice peaceful morning. Just the two of us and—hark! the soft crackle of my Puffa Puffa rice. 'Tis spring indeed. [*Slight pause.*] I suppose you think I'm cruel too, don't you? Well, I've damn good cause to be, haven't I? I mean, nobody's thought about my feelings, have they? It's all Annie— Annie—Annie . . . what about me? I was going to give her everything. Well, as much, as I could. My whole being. I wanted to make her happy for a weekend, that's all. I wanted to give her . . . [*Angrily*] It was only for a few hours for God's sake. Saturday night, back on Monday morning. That was all it was going to be. My God! The fuss. What about your wife, Norman? What about my wife? Don't you think I'd take Ruth away, just the same? If she'd come. But she won't. She has no need of me at all, that woman, except as an emotional punch bag . . . I tell you, if you gave Ruth a rose, she'd peel all the petals off to make sure there weren't any greenfly. And when she'd done that, she'd turn round and say, do you call that a rose? Look at it, it's all in bits. That's Ruth. If she came in now, she wouldn't notice me. She'd probably hang her coat on me . . . It's not fair, Reg. Look, I'll tell you. A man with my type of temperament should really be ideally square jawed, broad shouldered, have blue twinkling eyes, a chuckle in his voice and a spring in his stride. He should get through three women a day without even ruffling his hair. That's what I'm like inside. That's my appetite. That's me. I'm a three day man. There's enough of me in here to give. Not just sex, I'm talking about everything. The trouble is, I was born in the wrong damn body. Look at me. A gigolo trapped in a haystack. The tragedy of my life Norman Dewers—gigolo and assistant librarian. What's inside you, Reg? Apart from twelve bowls of cornflakes? What do you feel with Sarah? Do you sometimes feel like saying to her, no this is me. The real me. Look at me . . . [REG *finishes his cornflakes.*]

REG: I'll tell you something, Norman. You're a nice bloke. You've got your faults but you're a nice bloke but I think you must be the last person in the world I ever want to have breakfast with again.

NORMAN: Oh.

REG: No hard feelings you understand but . . .

[SARAH *enters looking pleased.*]

SARAH: Well, Norman. A little surprise for you.

NORMAN: Oh yes.

SARAH: Someone to see you.

NORMAN: Ruth?

SARAH: Just arrived. Isn't that nice? [*Turning to go off calling*] Ruth! [SARAH *goes out.*]

REG: [*alarmed*] Did someone say Ruth? Oh no . . . [*He rises, snatches a piece of toast and butters it hastily.*]

NORMAN: Tell her I'm not here, Tell her I'm . . .

[RUTH *enters. She is yelling the end of a conversation with* ANNIE *back in the kitchen.*]

RUTH: . . . I was pulled right out to the left, there was plenty of room for him to pass me. He had yards and yards, he just . . . [*Turning into the room*] Norman? Where is Norman?

NORMAN: Norman is here.

RUTH: [*peering shortsightedly*] Norman?—oh there you are.

REG: [*buttered toast in hand, heading for the other door*] Morning, Ruth. See you later.

[REG *goes out.*]

RUTH: [*continuing as if he was still in the room, fumbling in her bag*] Oh, Reg how are you? I've been meaning to ring you but I haven't had a minute, and how are those enchanting kids of yours? Little whatsername . . .?

NORMAN: He's gone.

RUTH: [*looking up, peering round the room*] What?

NORMAN: Reg has left the room. He's gone.

RUTH: Oh. Well, I was only being polite. I haven't seen him for ages . . .

NORMAN: You haven't seen anyone for ages. Why don't you wear your glasses?

RUTH: [*sitting*] Norman, what is going on here? What are you up to?

NORMAN: Since when have you cared what I'm up to?

RUTH: Well, I don't normally. You know you're perfectly free to come and go. Not that I could stop you. But I do object to having my Saturday nights ruined by all these bizarre phone calls. First of all, you ringing up screaming drunk—and then Sarah, practically at midnight, simply demanding I come down. Now what is going on?

NORMAN: You don't know?

RUTH: No. Is there anything to eat?

NORMAN: Sarah hasn't told you then?

RUTH: All she said was that you were here and that I ought to be here too. She sounded as if she was summoning relatives to your bedside . . .

NORMAN: I suppose she was, in a manner of speaking.

RUTH: I got quite worried.

NORMAN: Worried? Ha!

RUTH: What's that you're eating?

NORMAN: Since when do you worry about me?

RUTH: Of course I do. Now and then. Don't be tiresome. Is that cereal?

NORMAN: Puffa Puffa rice. [*Pushing the bowl to her*] Here, have it. After all you said to me about having no love for me—no feelings for me at all?

RUTH: Did I say that?

NORMAN: You know you did.

RUTH: No, I didn't.

NORMAN: It's imprinted on my brain . . .

RUTH: All I said was—is there any milk and sugar or do I have to eat these dry—all I said was . . .

NORMAN: It's got milk on . . .

RUTH: All I said was—that if you were all that unhappy with me—perhaps we ought to think of terminating our marriage . . .

NORMAN: [*excitedly*] Terminating it? You make it sound like a legal contract.

RUTH: That's exactly what it is, Norman. Don't be obtuse.

NORMAN: Marriage is more than that!

RUTH: Yes, all right, don't shout—

NORMAN: Marriage is sharing and giving and . . . things. Is that how you've seen us for five years? A legal contract? Some marriage. No confetti please—just throw sealing wax and red tape. Do you take this woman, hereinafter called the licensee of the first party . . .

RUTH: Norman, I can't go into all this now. Is there any sugar on this table?

NORMAN: And this man, hereinafter called the donor and sole giver . . .

RUTH: Norman, darling, do see if you can find the sugar.

NORMAN: [*rising and assembling everything in sight around RUTH*] Here. Tea, toast, marmalade, butter, knife, spoon, cup, saucer, hot water, sugar. All right?

RUTH: Thank you.

NORMAN: [*sinking back in a chair*] I don't think there's any hope for us. We're doomed.

RUTH: Norman. Can we talk quietly, please?

NORMAN: I doubt it.

RUTH: This is a perfect opportunity. We're on our own. We can sit here, talk, listen to each other's point of view and try and sort things out.

NORMAN: [*making an effort*] All right. I'll try. [*With sudden suppressed anger*] You are pouring hot water on your Puffa Puffa rice.

RUTH: [*absently*] What?

NORMAN: I told you they had milk on already. Why do you do that? You're always doing that. Why don't you look what you're doing?

RUTH: It doesn't matter.

NORMAN: If you'd only wear your glasses.

RUTH: I don't need glasses to eat cornflakes. I can see perfectly well, thank you. I just wasn't concentrating . . .

NORMAN: We're incompatible. We're damn well incompatible.

RUTH: I can see as well as you. It's only people I sometimes can't see very clearly.

NORMAN: Our house is knee deep in unused pairs of glasses.

RUTH: And most of the time that's preferable.

NORMAN: It's like a sale at an optician's.

RUTH: Norman . . .

NORMAN: Thousands of pairs of glasses.

RUTH: [angrily] Norman! [Taking a breath, calmly now] I have a great deal of work I should be doing at home. I have given that up. I have come down here because I was asked to come. I did not want to come. I want to stay as short a time as possible. Is that clear?

NORMAN: Oh yes. Got to get back to your work.

RUTH: Yes, I do. I have two full reports that have to be in tomorrow. If they are not in, I shall probably be fired. If I'm fired, we will have no money to pay the mortgage, no money for three-quarters of the gas and electricity bills . . .

NORMAN: All right, I'm a kept man. A married ponce.

RUTH: I don't mind keeping you. Not in the least. But I cannot continually chase after you all over the countryside. I just cannot spare the time, I'm sorry. As it is, you've held my career back about ten years. You interrupt me at meetings with embarrassing phone calls . . .

NORMAN: To tell you I love you, that's all. Is that wrong?

RUTH: You're continually bursting into my office when I'm seeing clients . . .

NORMAN: My God, is it wrong to love your wife?

RUTH: You behave abominably when I bring business friends home to dinner . . .

NORMAN: [snarling] What do they know about love?

RUTH: You have even been known to scrawl obscenities over my business papers.

NORMAN: All right, all right. I love you. I'm sorry.

RUTH: Yes, I love you too, Norman, but please leave me alone.

NORMAN: All right. In future, I'll whisper it quietly from Brazil. Would that suit you?

RUTH: All I'm saying is please try and see my point of view. Try and consider me.

NORMAN: I feel trapped. I'm a captive husband. That's what I am. [*He sinks his head in his hands.*]

RUTH: I have an awful feeling we haven't made much progress on that topic. Let's try another. What have you been doing down here to upset Sarah? I thought you had a conference.

NORMAN: Hah!

RUTH: Have you made a pass at her or something? Well, you'd better come home with me. You're not wanted here quite obviously. You can come home and mow the lawn.

NORMAN: Mow the lawn . . . Do you want to know what I'm doing here? I'll tell you, shall I?

RUTH: If you want to.

NORMAN: I will tell you. [*He rises.*]

RUTH: Where are you going?

NORMAN: Nowhere. I'm just standing up.

RUTH: Well, sit down, I can't see you properly.

NORMAN: This has to be said standing up.

RUTH: What is it, the National Anthem?

NORMAN: All right, you've had this coming . . . [*He pauses dramatically.*]

RUTH: Anyway, I discovered that they're what made me sneeze.

NORMAN: What are?

RUTH: My glasses. Whenever I wear them, I sneeze and my eyes run, so I can't see anything with them on anyway. I think they press on my sinus passages.

NORMAN: Vanity, that's what it is.

RUTH: It is not vanity. I am not vain.

NORMAN: Staring at yourself in the mirror all day long. Tarting yourself up for these so-called business associates.

RUTH: And I do not stare at myself in the mirror. For one thing I can't see myself properly without my glasses and because I can't bear looking at myself in glasses because I look so terrible in them, I never look at myself at all.

NORMAN: Do you want to hear what I have to say or don't you?

RUTH: Yes, all right. Just don't say I'm vain.

NORMAN: It concerns you, you know.

RUTH: It usually does.

NORMAN: There is someone else.

RUTH: What?

NORMAN: Whilst you have been engrossed in your financial wizardry . . . rigging the books for corrupt capitalist companies . . .

RUTH: Norman . . .

NORMAN: I very nearly, but for the grace of God and unforeseen circumstances, went off with another woman.

RUTH: You did?

NORMAN: Yes.

RUTH: Seriously?

NORMAN: Yes. I thought better of it in time. Thank heavens. Told her I wouldn't. But that was the reason behind this weekend. We had planned to go off together.

RUTH: For good?

NORMAN: No—probably not . . .

RUTH: Well, for how long?

NORMAN: Till Monday.

RUTH: Oh, I see. I thought you were a bit odd lately.

NORMAN: Odd?

RUTH: Well—quieter than usual. Who was it you were going with?

NORMAN: Does it matter?

RUTH: No. Since you didn't even go.

NORMAN: Do you want to know?

RUTH: Not if you don't want to tell me.
  [*Pause.*]

NORMAN: You want to know though, don't you?

RUTH: No, not really.
  [*Pause.*]

NORMAN: I'll tell you, shall I?

RUTH: You might as well.

NORMAN: Annie.

RUTH: Annie?

NORMAN: Yes.

RUTH: Oh Norman . . .

NORMAN: I thought that would shake you.

RUTH: I don't think I even believe you.

NORMAN: It's true.

RUTH: Not Annie. She's far too sensible.

NORMAN: We had planned a weekend together.

RUTH: You and Annie?

NORMAN: [*irritated*] Yes.

RUTH: Where?

NORMAN: East Grinstead.

RUTH: [*staring at him a second and then bursting into laughter*]
  Oh my God . . .

NORMAN: Don't laugh. It's true.
  [ANNIE *enters with a tray.*]
  Just the two of us together.

RUTH: [*laughing uncontrollably*] I have never heard anything
  so funny.

ANNIE: I'll clear this later, I'm sorry . . .

NORMAN: Annie! [*To* RUTH] Why won't you believe me?
  We were going away—together . . . Annie, you tell her,
  you tell her . . . You'd have lost me forever, do you know
  that?

ANNIE: Oh, Norman . . .

RUTH: [*drying her eyes*] I'm sorry—it's just East Grinstead . . .
  [*she starts laughing again.*]

NORMAN: All right, go on, laugh. We're in love.

[NORMAN *strides across to* ANNIE, *seizes her and her tray rather awkwardly and clasps her to him.*]

Don't you care? We're in love . . .

[SARAH *comes in with a second tray. She stops in the doorway.*]

ANNIE: [*struggling, muffled as she is clasped to* NORMAN's *bosom*] Norman, don't . . .

NORMAN: We're in love . . .

[RUTH *continues to laugh.* SARAH, *surveying the scene, looks on horrified.*]

Curtain

ACT TWO

SCENE ONE

The dining room. Sunday evening, 8 p.m. ANNIE *alone putting knives and forks away in sideboard.* NORMAN *creeps in.*

NORMAN: [*in a whisper*] Annie.

ANNIE: [*jumping*] Oh, don't do that. Frightened me to death.

NORMAN: [*whispering*] Hallo.

ANNIE: [*whispering*] Hallo. What are you doing?

NORMAN: [*whispering*] Wanted to see you alone.

ANNIE: [*whispering*] Why are we whispering?

NORMAN: [*whispering*] Them.

ANNIE: [*normally*] They can't hear us.

NORMAN: [*loudly*] Oh, Annie, I need you. [*He moves to her.*]

ANNIE: Ssh. [*She pulls away*] Norman . . .

NORMAN: What's wrong?

ANNIE: Nothing. Just don't . . .

NORMAN: Why not? Have you gone off me?

ANNIE: Well, slightly—no. You know . . .

NORMAN: What do you mean, slightly?

ANNIE: [*confused*] Oh . . .

NORMAN: What?

ANNIE: Well, it's ridiculous now. Tom's here. Ruth's here. Stop playing games.

NORMAN: Oh, it's a game now, is it? When we planned this weekend it was no game. It was going to be an adventure. An experience for both of us.

ANNIE: But we didn't plan to spend it here, did we? Anyway it's all gone wrong. Everybody knows including Ruth.

NORMAN: Ruth? I wouldn't worry about her. She laughed. Can you imagine that, laughing . . .

ANNIE: She was right. It was absurd. I don't think Tom's laughing, mind you.

NORMAN: Tom. Who cares what he thinks?

ANNIE: I do.

NORMAN: You do?

ANNIE: Yes.

NORMAN: I thought he didn't matter to you.

ANNIE: I never said that.

NORMAN: You implied . . .

ANNIE: No.

NORMAN: What about me? I mean, us

ANNIE: [*sharp*] What about us, Norman?

NORMAN: I see. That's me finished with, is it? As far as you're concerned. Chucked away like an empty bottle. That's my lot.

ANNIE: Yes.

NORMAN: God, you're cruel.

ANNIE: Yes.

NORMAN: I expect it's because of last night, isn't it?

ANNIE: Not really.

NORMAN: That's why you're angry with me. Because I got drunk. But I got drunk because of you, don't you see? I was unhappy so I got drunk. I'm sorry.

ANNIE: Doesn't bother me.

NORMAN: I got disgustingly drunk.

ANNIE: You can get as drunk as you like, it doesn't bother me.

NORMAN: Oh, great. Would you mind if I dropped dead?

ANNIE: That's entirely up to you.

NORMAN: Oh fine. That's fine. [*He ponders*] You're getting bitter. Did you know that? You used to be innocent and pure and fragile.

ANNIE: Oh balls. I'm sorry, Norman, but balls. You do talk rubbish. No one can spend five years looking after that cantankerous woman upstairs and remain innocent and pure. And after lugging her in and out of bed single-handed, day in day out, I'm the last person in this world you'd call fragile. I mean, look at me, Norman, do I look even remotely fragile?

NORMAN: I meant mentally fragile.

ANNIE: That sounds even worse. Makes me sound like a half-wit.

NORMAN: I don't know what's got into you. You've been corrupted.

ANNIE: I'm sick to death of being used, Norman.

NORMAN: I think I must have corrupted you, somehow.

ANNIE: You and Ruth will have to play on your own. Don't use me as ammunition.

NORMAN: And cynical. I never thought you'd get like that. I think it's my fault. [*Pause.*] So you're going back to Tom?

ANNIE: I'm not going back to anyone. I just want to be left alone. I've had you shoving me, Sarah shoving me, Ruth sniggering. I'll be glad when you've all gone home. I really will. I'm sorry.

NORMAN: I think I've got one of my depressions coming on again. I came in here for comfort.

ANNIE: Well go and see Ruth.

NORMAN: All right. Back to the living death, eh?

ANNIE: Oh, Norman. You make me so angry.

NORMAN: All right. I'll go. I know when I'm not wanted. I'll go back where I'm not wanted. I'll go. Goodbye.

ANNIE: [*infuriated, picking up a vase threateningly*] I warn you, I'll—

NORMAN: Go on. Go on. What have I got to live for?
[ANNIE *screams in frustration. She bangs down the vase.* TOM *enters.*]

TOM: Ah.

ANNIE: Hallo, Tom.

TOM: Hallo.
[*They stand for a moment in silence.*]

NORMAN: Well, I can see I'm in the way. If you'll excuse me, I'm just off to look for a length of rope.

ANNIE: You are not in anyone's way but your own. I'm going to start dinner. Excuse me both of you.
[ANNIE *goes out.*]

NORMAN: It must be your after-shave.

TOM: Um?

NORMAN: That drives them away.

TOM: Oh. Look here, Norman. You're a very good fellow.

NORMAN: Thank you.

TOM: I've always thought of you as a good fellow. However. This is difficult to say without hurting your feelings. I don't think you're a very good influence on Annie.

NORMAN: Really?

TOM: I've heard all about this business of your going away. I've also observed you this weekend. I don't think I like it at all. It's upsetting her and that's not right. The point is, if it happens again . . . well, I used to do boxing. I didn't enjoy it and I wasn't at all good. I couldn't get out of it, you see. It was compulsory at our school. But I did learn to throw a pretty useful punch. So.

NORMAN: Am I being threatened?

TOM: Yes.

NORMAN: My God, I'm being threatened.

[SARAH *comes in.*]

I am being threatened.

SARAH: About time.

NORMAN: Hah!

SARAH: [*calling*] Reg!

TOM: Excuse me.

[TOM *goes out.*]

NORMAN: That man's turned homicidal.

SARAH: I think as far as you're concerned, we all have to a certain extent, Norman.

NORMAN: Sarah. You don't hate me, do you? I mean, I know perhaps you disapprove but you don't hate me?

SARAH: No, I don't hate you, Norman.

NORMAN: Thank you. Thank you for that, at least.

SARAH: But I can't say I like you very much, most of the time.

NORMAN: All right. All right, I'm going . . .

SARAH: Norman.

NORMAN: What?

SARAH: Will you do something for me?

NORMAN: What?

SARAH: Will you try, just for this evening, not to start any more scenes or arguments?

NORMAN: Me?

SARAH: I'd like, just for once, all of us to get through an evening—as a family. I don't know if you've realized it, Norman, but I have had a lot of nervous trouble in the past. And every time I come down here, I have a relapse. When I get home from this house, I find I'm shaking all over. For days. And I get these rashes up the insides of my arms.

NORMAN: My goodness.

SARAH: Now it's not fair on me, Norman. I have a family to look after, a house to run.

NORMAN: Yes, yes of course.

SARAH: Well.

NORMAN: Yes. Your trouble is you're over-emotional.

SARAH: Very possibly.

NORMAN: You're like me.

SARAH: Are you sure I am?

NORMAN: We feel. We've got nerve-endings sticking out of our heads. We've no cynicism or scepticism to act as shock absorbers. Everything that is, that happens becomes part of us. We're probably a new race. Had you thought of that? Born too early.

SARAH: All I'm saying is, if there's too much noise, I get these headaches.

NORMAN: We're not understood. None of that lot out there understand us. They're all bogged down in their own little lives.

SARAH: Yes . . .

NORMAN: Self obsessed. Annie, Tom, Ruth—even Reg. Don't worry, Sarah.

SARAH: What?

NORMAN: This evening's going to be all right.

SARAH: Is it?

NORMAN: We'll both go flat out together to make it a success.

SARAH: Oh yes?

NORMAN: For God's sake, this is a family. We should care. If we don't care, brothers sisters, husbands wives . . . if we can't finally join hands, what hope is there for anybody? Make it a banquet, Sarah my love, make it a banquet.

SARAH: There's nothing in the larder.

NORMAN: Improvise. We can improvise. What do we need? [*He rushes to the sideboard and grabs handfuls of cutlery indiscriminately from the drawer*] Knifes—forks—spoons— [*He scatters them on the table.*]

SARAH: Yes, all right Norman, I'll do it.

NORMAN: [*producing linen*] Table napkins.

SARAH: No, Norman, those are traycloths. I'll do it, don't worry please.

NORMAN: All right. I've started you off, I'll leave it to you. I'll go and change.

SARAH: Change?

NORMAN: For dinner.

SARAH: Change into what?

NORMAN: I'll find something. I'll improvise, Sarah, improvise. It's like an old clothes shop upstairs.

SARAH: Annie should have cleared it out. There's her father's clothes still in the wardrobe. There'll be moths.

NORMAN: Quite right.

[*NORMAN goes to the door and passes REG coming in.*]
Evening Reg, old sport.
[*NORMAN slaps REG on the back and exits.*]

REG: What's up with him?

SARAH: Oh, there you are.

REG: He's very cheerful. That looks ominous.

SARAH: I think I've persuaded him to make an effort this evening. I think I have. Would you see if you can find the mats in the drawer.

REG: What sort of effort?

SARAH: To avoid hysterical scenes. To behave in a civilized manner.

REG: [*at sideboard*] Ha—ha—ha.

SARAH: I pray that for once we might get through the evening without one angry word. I want us to have a quiet meal, to be able to go into the lounge afterwards, sit down all six of us, and enjoy each other's company like a family.

REG: Are you aware who the six people are? Norman to name but five. And Ruth. That's a civil war to start with. Don't ask for the impossible. Just pray we're still alive tomorrow morning. That'll do for a start.

SARAH: I mean, if a family can't care about each other, what hope is there for the rest of the . . . I'll never forgive you if you don't try. I mean it, Reg. I know you find it all very amusing—Ruth and Norman continually bickering, Annie behaving like a tramp . . .

REG: What?

SARAH: You've seen how she's been dressed all day. Tarted up like that, it doesn't suit her, it never did.

REG: You're always on she doesn't bother.

SARAH: She doesn't have to go the other way, does she? Why can't she wear something nice and simple and— plain . . .? All that make up on. I mean, it's not even fashionable. Especially when you know who she's done it for.

REG: Tom, I should think.

SARAH: Tom? For Norman. She's set her sights at him and he's enjoying every minute of it. Playing one sister off against the other . . . Well, any more of this and you know what'll happen? What always happens when I come down here.

REG: Oh no? You've not got the shakes again, have you?

SARAH: You ought to know me by now, Reg. I can't bear these sort of atmospheres.

REG: It's not your back, is it?

SARAH: Not at the moment. But the way I've had to run round trying to cope with one crisis after another . . .

REG: Well, sit down. Have a rest for a second.

SARAH: [*snapping*] How can I sit down? Be sensible. How can I possibly sit down?

REG: [*snapping back*] All right, stand up. Suit yourself. I'm only trying to be . . . You want these mats?

SARAH: Yes, I said I did.

REG: [*studying them*] Marvellous, these are, every picture tells a story.

SARAH: We're going to need two more chairs. I'm sure there used to be six of these. Heaven knows what she's done with them.

REG: All right, I'll look for chairs. Don't worry, keep calm. It'll be all right.

[ANNIE *enters.*]

ANNIE: Well, I've scraped together what there is. It should just about feed us all. Opened every tin we had and poured them into a saucepan. Made a sort of gluey stew. Then there's the salad we can finish . . .

REG: Oh, good grief. Not again.

ANNIE: It works out about one lettuce leaf each.

REG: Thank heaven for that.

SARAH: Well done. Didn't you have six of these chairs at one time? I'm sure at Christmas . . .

ANNIE: Oh yes, they fell to bits.

SARAH: Fell to bits?

ANNIE: Everything does that in this house. Woodworm or old age.

REG: You should get that treated.

ANNIE: Old age, you mean?

REG: Ah well, I don't know about that. Father used to say, the only thing for old age is a brave face, a good tailor and comfortable shoes. Chairs . . .

ANNIE: I should use the ones in the sitting room. There's a couple there with legs.

REG: Right.

[REG *goes out.*]

ANNIE: You're using the mats?

SARAH: Yes, I thought we'd—

ANNIE: Bit posh. We only use those on Mother's birthday.

SARAH: Well, I thought we'd do something a little special since we're all here. Nice that Ruth could come.

ANNIE: Yes.

SARAH: It makes it complete. And it means that Norman won't be left out.

ANNIE: Yes.

SARAH: I really do like that dress.

ANNIE: Thank you. It's pretty old but it's a good standby.

SARAH: Yes . . . Anyway, I thought we'd have a really cosy family meal together. Try and make it a happy evening.

ANNIE: Super.

[REG *enters with a chair.*]

REG: Here's one of them.

SARAH: We need two.

REG: All right, all right. I'm going back for the other. Tom's sitting on it.

SARAH: Well, move him off it.

REG: [*going out*] You ever tried moving Tom?

[REG *goes out as* RUTH *enters.*]

RUTH: Somebody's saucepan seems to be getting rather agitated out there.

SARAH: Did you turn it down?

RUTH: No. I whispered soothing words to it. Of course, I turned it down.

ANNIE: I'll see to it.

SARAH: All right. I'll go. I'll go. [*With a glare at* RUTH] If you want something doing in this house, you might as well do it yourself.

[SARAH *goes out.*]

RUTH: My God, Mother's mats. Is it a birth, a death or a marriage?

ANNIE: She's doing the lot. I mean, she's not actually doing anything but she's organizing the lot.

RUTH: What on earth for, silly cow? Who's going to notice?

ANNIE: I think this is her attempt at a grand reunion. A cosy family meal with Sarah presiding.

RUTH: Oh no. Have we all got to sit round with fixed grins? . . . It's Christmas all over again. I thought I'd come in here, so I wouldn't embarrass your fiancé or whatever he is. He can't bear to look me in the face.

ANNIE: Poor Tom.

RUTH: It was rather unfortunate. Believe it or not, I was attempting unsuccessfully to give him lessons on how to woo you. Tom being Tom assumed I was giving him lessons on how to woo me. I managed to load him all right but I pointed him in the wrong direction. It was silly of me to interfere, I'm sorry. Serves me right. I'll leave it to Sarah in future. I mean, I don't know you may not even care for the man. You've never really said one way or the other. We've always assumed you and Tom, Tom and you. Presumably you wouldn't have him round here at all if you didn't. You do like him, don't you?

ANNIE: Yes. I'm very fond of him.

RUTH: I think he's in love with you. As far as one can fathom. It's just he's so—well, one could be nice and say deep. Except if you say someone's deep, it more or less implies there's something at the bottom. I'm not so sure with Tom.

ANNIE: Oh, you'd be surprised.

RUTH: All he needs is a shove. Somebody needs to do it. Anybody. Except Norman that is. Whose sole advice to Tom was to throw punches at you.

ANNIE: Norman told him to do that?

RUTH: It's Norman's answer to female psychology. He's very subtle. Have you noticed? Well, you probably have. You nearly fell for it.

ANNIE: I'm sorry. I never for a minute intended to take Norman away from you or anything.

RUTH: Forget it. You couldn't possibly take Norman away from me. That assumes I own him in the first place. I've never done that. I always feel with Norman that I have him on loan from somewhere. Like one of his library books. I'll get a card one day informing me he's overdue and there's a fine to pay on him. Oh, I should have gone back to town this afternoon. I'm going to have to phone the office tomorrow and plead illness. Again. Of all the working days lost in this country over the year, half are due to strikes and illness and the other half to people chasing after Norman.

[REG *comes on with the other chair.*]

REG: Got it. He moved. Tom moved. Got the chair.

RUTH: Have you seen Norman? I don't like it when I can't see him. Where is he?

REG: Oh, he was shouting about out there. Said something about going up to change.

ANNIE: He's got nothing to change into.

RUTH: That won't stop him. He'll probably come down in a counterpane.

ANNIE: Oh, goodness, would you . . .

RUTH: I'll try . . .

[RUTH *goes out passing* SARAH *returning with a bottle of home made wine.*]

SARAH: Don't go too far away, Ruth. Nearly ready. I've left the stew to simmer, Annie. Reg, would you call everyone. Tom and Norman.

REG: Right you are. [*Going to door and yelling*] Tom! Norman!

SARAH: [*wincing*] Please, there's no need to shout. Go and fetch them.

REG: Sorry. [*Whispering*] Tom. Norman.

SARAH: Reg—

REG: All right. All right . . .

[REG *goes out.* TOM *comes in the other door.*]

TOM: Somebody call? [*Sighting the table*] Aha, this looks promising.

TOM: Very smart. Napkins, mats, wine—so on.

SARAH: And tonight, that wine is strictly rationed.

TOM: Ah.

SARAH: If you could open it, Tom, it would be most helpful. [SARAH *goes out.*]

TOM: Right. [*He starts to do so*] Two meals in two days. Not doing badly, am I?

ANNIE: About average.

TOM: I think I've sorted things out with Norman.

ANNIE: Have you?

TOM: Sent him off with a flea in his ear, I'm afraid.

ANNIE: Oh. Tom . . .

TOM: Um?

ANNIE: We've all made a sort of agreement that we're going to try and not have any rows or anything tonight. It's for Sarah's sake really. A really happy meal, you know. So do your bit won't you?

TOM: What, you mean jokes and things?

ANNIE: No, not necessarily.

TOM: Oh good, I'm awfully bad at jokes. I forget the ending.

ANNIE: No, well—I know you never do—but don't complain or cause any trouble, will you?

TOM: Lord, no. Just get my food down me. That's all I'm here for. You know me.

ANNIE: [*doubtfully*] Yes . . .
[SARAH *re-enters with a tray of plates adorned with sparse salad.*]

SARAH: Come along. It's all ready. Where is everyone? [*Calling*] Reg—
[REG *enters.*]

REG: Can't find either of them. [*Seeing* TOM] Ah, there you are. No sign of Norman, he's vanished.

SARAH: Well, all right, we won't wait. Let's get seated. Reg, you go up the end there, would you?

REG: Up the end.

SARAH: And Tom, you come next to me here, would you?
[RUTH *enters.*]

RUTH: Norman's in the bathroom.

SARAH: Oh well . . .

RUTH: From the sound of it, he's washing. He's so ashamed of the fact, he's locked the door. [*She sits.*]

SARAH: Oh well, he'll be down I expect . . . no, not there, Ruth dear. Would you mind sitting one seat further up?

RUTH: [*moving grudgingly*] Oh, really . . .

ANNIE: Where am I sitting?

SARAH: [*to* TOM *who is still wandering*] You're here, Tom. Sit here.

REG: [*offering* ANNIE *his own chair*] Annie, you should be sitting here. You're the hostess.

ANNIE: [*sitting*] Right.

SARAH: No, she can't sit there. She's out of order.

REG: She's the hostess. She should sit at the head.

SARAH: But then we've got two women sitting together.

RUTH: I'll move back down here then. That's easy enough.

SARAH: [*stopping her*] No, Ruth, no. Stay where you are.

REG: Now I'll go here next to Annie. Then it's right. [*He sits*].

TOM: No, it's not. You're next to me.

SARAH: [*getting agitated*] Now, we've got two men together. Why don't you leave it to me?

REG: It's all right, it's all right. Don't get excited. Now, Tom, you move round one and sit at the end there.

TOM: [*going to do so*] Right ho.

RUTH: Would it be easier if I ate in the kitchen?

REG: Just a second. Do you mind, Ruth, do you mind?

SARAH: Don't sit there, Tom. That's my chair.

TOM: Oh, I'm sorry, I thought he said . . . [TOM *moves one chair further round.*]

REG: Now, we want a girl over here. Ruth. Over here.

RUTH: I don't want to worry you but you've got a woman at both ends of the table.

SARAH: That's what I'm saying. Why won't you listen?

REG: No, no, look. We've got Ruth, there—then me—then Annie—Norman over there, when he comes and Tom next to—ah, that's where we're wrong. Tom, you're in the wrong seat.

TOM: [*jumping up guiltily*] Sorry. I thought she said . . .

RUTH: I am about to sit down permanently.

SARAH: Reg, will you listen?

REG: Tom, you're supposed to be at the end.

SARAH: Reg—

TOM: I've just been moved from there.

RUTH: I am sitting down—now.

REG: Look, do as you're told and go to the end.

SARAH: [*screaming*] Reg, will you kindly leave this to me.

REG: I am simply trying—

ANNIE: [*hissing*] Reg.

REG: What? All right love, all right. I leave it to you. I was only trying to help. Everybody go where Sarah tells them.

SARAH: Thank you. Tom. You are sitting here.

TOM: Aha. Back where I started.

SARAH: Reg at the top.

REG: That's wrong, you know . . .

SARAH: At the top. Ruth.

RUTH: I have sat down. I refuse to get up.

ANNIE: [*hissing*] Ruth.

SARAH: Ruth, you're all right where you are.

[NORMAN *enters, now dressed in an old, ill-fitting suit and collar and tie.*]

NORMAN: Evening.

SARAH: [*aghast*] Norman.

[REG *laughs.* SARAH *glares.*]

ANNIE: Ssh.

[REG *stops laughing.*]

NORMAN: I heard we were dressing for dinner. Good evening. Carry on, talk among yourselves. [*He sits.*]

[NORMAN *is now sat between* REG *at the top of the table and* TOM, *who is on a very low chair indeed.*]

SARAH: No, Norman, not there.

REG: Is that my father's suit, you've got on?

NORMAN: If he was a man with extraordinary arm and inside leg measurements, yes indeed.

SARAH: Norman, not there.

NORMAN: Why not here?

ANNIE: [*hissing*] Norman.

SARAH: Because it's wrong.

NORMAN: Wrong? Is it wrong to sit between my old pal Reg and this dwarf on my left? [*Patting the top of* TOM'*s head*] Hallo, little chap.

TOM: Hallo.

RUTH: [*hissing*] Norman.

SARAH: Norman!

ANNIE: It's all right, Sarah. I'll sit here. It's fine.

SARAH: But—

ANNIE: This is fine.

REG: Fine.

RUTH: Fine.

SARAH: Oh, well. It's not correct.

NORMAN: Is this lettuce leaf all for me? I can hardly believe my good fortune.

ANNIE: [*hissing*] Norman.

[*A pause.*]

SARAH: Well . . .

[*A pause.*]

REG: [*suddenly*] Talking of animals . . .

[*People look up in surprise.*]

Another amusing story about a vet for you, Tom.

TOM: Oh.

REG: There's this Englishman and this Italian, you see, standing by a lake.

NORMAN: That's unusual.

REG: And anyway, they see this dog fall in the water, you see—nearly drowning—coughing and spluttering—nearly drowning.

NORMAN: Woof—splutter splutter—woof woof.

REG: Thank you, Norman. Yes. Well, the Italian dives in,

rescues the dog, brings it back to the shore, lays it out, gives it mouth to mouth respiration . . .

NORMAN: Uggh.

REG: Twenty seconds, the dog's perfectly all right. The Englishman says, that's wonderful. Are you a vet? The Italian says, am I a vet? I'm a-soaking vet, what do you think? [*He coughs.*]

[NORMAN *laughs. The others manage faint smiles. Silence.*]

NORMAN: I liked that. Subtle foreign joke. Did you get that, Tom?

TOM: Yes, I think so.

NORMAN: Thought it might have been above your head. [*He laughs.*]

ANNIE: [*hissing*] Norman.

NORMAN: Above your head . . .

RUTH: Norman.

[RUTH *aims a kick at* NORMAN *but kicks* REG. REG *jumps.*] I'm sorry.

NORMAN: This lettuce is superb. Whoever cooked this has a knack with lettuce. It's a triumph.

[*A pause.*]

SARAH: Are you all right there, Tom? You're terribly low.

TOM: No, I'm fine.

SARAH: Do you want to fetch a—?

TOM: [*anxiously*] No, no, no.

SARAH: We've been very lucky with the weather.

ALL: Yes.

NORMAN: True, true. [*Pause.*] Could have been raining, couldn't it?

SARAH: Yes.

[*A pause.*]

NORMAN: Or even snowing. [*Pause.*] Snow in July. Unusual but you never know these days, do you? I mean, we must be thankful for small mercies, in my opinion. If this was Australia, this would be mid-winter. Think of that. Thick snow on the koolibah trees, koala bears rushing about in gum boots . . .

RUTH: Norman, just sit quietly and enjoy your lettuce.

NORMAN: [*in an undertone*] I'm making small talk.

RUTH: Yes. Well, it's not quite small enough, dear.

NORMAN: I can't get it any smaller. I'll swallow it.
[*A pause.*]

TOM: Excuse me . . .

SARAH: Yes, Tom?

TOM: Er—salt.

SARAH: Pass Tom the salt, Norman.

NORMAN: Salt. Certainly. Here we are, little fellow. You enjoying eating with the grown-ups, are you? Long past your bedtime.

TOM: Oh, do put a bun in it, Norman, there's a good chap.

NORMAN: A bun. I should be so lucky.

SARAH: Why don't you get a cushion, Tom?

TOM: [*irritably*] No.

SARAH: All right, all right. I was only suggesting . . .

TOM: Sorry.
[*A pause.*]

ANNIE: Everyone finished? I'll get the rest.

SARAH: Tom hasn't quite finished.

TOM: All right, all right. Don't worry about me.

RUTH: Do you mean to say there's more?

ANNIE: Just some stew so called.

RUTH: Well, I'll try and squeeze it in.

ANNIE: Look, if you want to take over and try and do any better . . .

RUTH: All right, sorry.

ANNIE: Sitting there on your backside complaining.

RUTH: Who's complaining? It's a feast.

SARAH: [*shrilly*] Don't let's quarrel, please.

REG: Plates. Let's have the plates, everybody.
[REG *stacks his,* RUTH's *and* NORMAN's *plates and gives them to* ANNIE.]

ANNIE: Thank you. Won't be a second.
[ANNIE *goes out.*]

SARAH: Reg . . .

REG: Mm?

SARAH: Offer to help.

REG: Oh, all right. Does she need it?

SARAH: She's doing it all on her own.

REG: All right.

[REG *goes out.*]

SARAH: Now, would somebody like to pour us some wine?

NORMAN: Certainly. Certainly. My pleasure . . .

RUTH: This meal is rapidly becoming unbearable.

NORMAN: [*offering wine*] Sarah?

SARAH: Thank you, Norman. Just a little drop.

[NORMAN *continues pouring wine around the table.*]

RUTH: Why don't you take a tranquilliser and go to bed, Sarah? Leave us to fight in peace.

SARAH: Because there is no reason to fight.

RUTH: None of us happen to like each other very much. I think that's a very good reason.

NORMAN: Speak for yourself. I am full of love this evening.

RUTH: Just for yourself? Or is anyone else included?

SARAH: Ignore her, Norman, ignore her.

NORMAN: I will, Sarah, I will.

TOM: Ah!

NORMAN: Hallo, Junior.

TOM: I just remember it. A joke.

RUTH: Oh, God.

SARAH: Oh, a joke, Tom. That's nice.

TOM: Quite a funny one really.

SARAH: Go on, Tom.

TOM: Er—well—it's about these two missionaries. And they're in Africa, you see and—no, three missionaries, sorry—and they were—

SARAH: In Africa, yes.

TOM: I think it was Africa. Doesn't really matter, really. Anyway . . .

[ANNIE *enters carrying the stew in a saucepan, followed by* REG *with a pile of soup plates.*

ANNIE: Here we are. Thought we'd better use soup plates. It's very runny. It's mostly tinned soup anyway.

SARAH: Couldn't you have used the dish?

ANNIE: This is all right. Nobody minds a saucepan. Just more washing up otherwise. Do you want to dish up or shall I?

SARAH: No, no, that's all right.

TOM: And there was this tribe of very wild cannibals.

ANNIE: Cannibals? Where?

TOM: In Africa, I think.

ANNIE: What's he talking about?

RUTH: He's telling us a joke.

ANNIE: Oh no, Tom love, you don't need to. Honestly.

NORMAN: It's a funny one.

SARAH: Quiet. Let Tom tell his joke.

ANNIE: [*starting to dish up*] I hope there's enough to go around.

TOM: And the first missionary says, look here I'm going to try and convert these very wild cannibals to Christianity. You see. And off he goes—through the jungle . . .

ANNIE: [*to* RUTH] Can you pass this to Reg?

NORMAN: Good health, friends.

TOM: Through the jungle—for days and days . . .

ANNIE: [*handing plate to* RUTH] Ruth.

REG: What are these white lumps?

ANNIE: Tinned potatoes, probably.

REG: Oh.

ANNIE: Could be tinned pears. I lost count.

TOM: And eventually he comes to this village which is full of these very wild cannibals dancing about . . .

NORMAN: Woolla—woolla—woolla.

ANNIE: That's for Norman. I hope it's hot enough.

RUTH: What on earth do you call this?

ANNIE: Sloppy stew. Take it or leave it. Tom . . .

TOM: [*taking his plate*] Thank you very much. And as soon as they see him, they grab hold of him and put him in the cooking pot.

NORMAN: This is a very tall story for a short man.

ANNIE: Sarah—oh, I've run out. I gave Reg too much. Reg . . .

RUTH: You can have mine.

ANNIE: No, I gave Reg too much. Pass your plate down, Reg.

REG: Ah. Some more is there?

RUTH: No. Less.

REG: Less?

ANNIE: I miscalculated. Sorry.

REG: Well, I didn't get all that much.

SARAH: You had more than anybody else. Pass your plate. I'm sorry, you were saying, Tom?

TOM: Yes. And the chief of these very wild cannibals says . . .

ANNIE: Sorry, Reg, fair shares for all.

RUTH: You're welcome to mine.

REG: We're in no danger of overeating.

TOM: I think I'm giving this story up.

SARAH: You eat far too much anyway. Do you good.

TOM: Nobody seems to be listening.

NORMAN: I'm listening, little friend.

REG: I'll be glad to get home for a meal.

SARAH: It's all right for you, you don't have to cook it, do you? Think of me for a change—

ANNIE: This isn't bad, considering. Like oxtail soup with unidentified lumps.

SARAH: Think of it as a rest for me. I mean, what rest do I get at home? Not only you to look after but the children as well.

RUTH: If you didn't want children, you shouldn't have had them.

SARAH: I never said I didn't want them, Ruth.

RUTH: You're always making out they're some dreadful burden. Like a penance. You never seem to enjoy them.

SARAH: It's very difficult to talk to someone who's never had any children.

RUTH: Through choice. Through choice.

NORMAN: Your choice.

RUTH: Certainly my choice.

SARAH: And very one-sided it is by the sound of it.

RUTH: No more than yours probably was. I mean, did you honestly consult Reg as to whether he wanted children?

SARAH: Of course I did.

ANNIE: Biologically impossible not to, I should think.

RUTH: I simply cannot bear this blind pig-headed assumption that you're a totally unfulfilled second class woman until you've had children.

SARAH: I never said that.

NORMAN: May I say a word here?—

RUTH: You imply it. You use those children like some awful weapon. I alone who have borne children know the true meaning of suffering.

NORMAN: Hear! Hear!

SARAH: I don't know what you're talking about. That's absolute nonsense. I mean, it's no business of mine if you choose to deny yourself one of the greatest satisfactions...

RUTH: There you go again. Denying myself. What's the matter with the woman?

REG: Hey, hey.

SARAH: I might well ask what was the matter with you?

RUTH: There is nothing whatever the matter with me.

NORMAN: May I put in a word for the rational man?

RUTH: No, you may not. We've heard quite enough from you for one weekend.

NORMAN: So much for the rational man.

RUTH: By all means have your children. I'm not asking you to deny yourself as you put it. All I'm saying is, for God's sake don't stand about looking martyred once you've had them. And don't look down your nose at the rest of us.

SARAH: I'm not prepared to get into another argument over this, Ruth. You don't know what you're talking about. You never will.

RUTH: She is so dogmatic. Reg, I feel sorry for you. How

do you live with a woman like this who's so pigheaded?
She just will not listen.

SARAH: Listen . . .

RUTH: She will not listen to a single word.

SARAH: Will you listen to me for a minute? If I feel sorry
for anyone, it's Norman.

NORMAN: A blow for the rational man.

SARAH: Have you ever consulted him? Of course you
haven't. You've just gone selfishly ahead with your own
career . . .

RUTH: While you're busy manufacturing lots more little
Reggies and Sarahs. What a wonderful contribution that
is.

SARAH: Oh well, if we're going to get personal.

RUTH: If that isn't selfishness and conceit of the worst sort,
I don't know what is. [*Banging down her spoon angrily*] And
this is absolutely revolting, I don't know how anyone can
eat it.

[RUTH *pushes her bowl angrily from her. It knocks* REG's *wine
glass and spills the contents over his trousers.*]

REG: [*jumping up angrily*] Oh, for crying out loud.

RUTH: I'm sorry. I'm sorry. Here—[*she flings her napkin at
him.*]

REG: Look at these trousers. Why the hell don't you watch
what you're doing?

SARAH: All right. Don't make a fuss.

REG: What?

SARAH: Don't start losing your temper over a little thing
like that.

REG: Now, don't you start on about people losing their
tempers. If anyone's got a temper in this room, we know
who that is.

SARAH: I don't know how you have the nerve to say that.

NORMAN: May I interrupt here?

REG: I'm going to change these. I'm soaking.

SARAH: It wouldn't be surprising if I did have a temper
living with you.

NORMAN: Without displaying any prejudice, my wife is obviously to blame for this.

RUTH: Norman, don't you start.

NORMAN: She is the original irrational woman.

ANNIE: Norman.

REG: I am going to change my trousers. [*He goes out.*]

NORMAN: She has no feelings of womanhood, let alone motherhood.

ANNIE: Norman.

RUTH: You really do ask for it, don't you?

NORMAN: And you're jealous of those that have.

ANNIE: Norman.

RUTH: You just say one more thing, Norman.

NORMAN: You've got as much feeling as a dried up tea bag.

SARAH: [*shrilly*] Stop it.

ANNIE: Norman.

TOM: [*rising*] Right. That's quite enough from you.

NORMAN: Eh?

TOM: I warned you, Norman.

[TOM *launches an unexpected blow at* NORMAN. NORMAN *falls off his chair.*]

ANNIE: Tom!

SARAH: [*drumming on the table with her fists*] Stop it! Stop it! Stop it!

TOM: There.

RUTH: Serve you right.

TOM: I warned you. I warned him, you know.

NORMAN: What did you do that for?

TOM: I did warn you. I said if you upset Annie any more. I'm afraid I can't sit by and have her called names by you.

NORMAN: What names?

TOM: Well, you called her a—teabag or something. That is not on. I won't have that.

NORMAN: You fool. I wasn't talking to her.

TOM: What?

NORMAN: I was talking to my wife.

TOM: Oh. Were you? Oh, that's rather different.

RUTH: Oh thank you. Meaning I am an old teabag, I suppose.

TOM: No, I didn't mean that.

RUTH: Oh, to hell with the lot of you.

[RUTH *storms out*.]

NORMAN: You great idiot.

TOM: I'm very sorry. I thought you were talking to Annie.

NORMAN: You great stupid—vet.

TOM: [*trying to help him*] I really am terribly—Can I—?

NORMAN: Oh, go away. Just go away.

TOM: Yes, yes of course. I'm sorry. [*Turning in the doorway*] Misunderstanding, you see. Oh gosh.

[TOM *goes out*.]

ANNIE: Tom . . . Oh Norman, how could you?

[ANNIE *follows* TOM *out*. SARAH *sits in a state near to traumatic shock. She is visibly shaking.* NORMAN *rises*.]

NORMAN: Lunatic . . . [*He paces about*.]

SARAH: This is the last time I do anything for this family.

NORMAN: Do you know he could have killed me? If I'd fallen awkwardly. If I'd fallen that way instead of this way—I'd have broken my neck. Sobering thought. But who would have cared, Sarah? Who would have cared?

SARAH: How could they? How could they do it? How could they behave like that?

NORMAN: We are misunderstood people, Sarah. Misunderstood. [*He pats her head*.]

SARAH: [*suddenly lunging and clinging to him*] Oh Norman.

NORMAN: We are definitely misunderstood.

Curtain

ACT TWO

Scene Two

The dining room. 8 a.m. Monday morning. ANNIE *comes in with a tray of breakfast things. She is now dressed as before in Act One Scene One. She starts to lay the table.* SARAH *comes in.*

SARAH: Oh—

ANNIE: Morning.

SARAH: You're already doing it.

ANNIE: Yes.

SARAH: I was going to get breakfast.

ANNIE: Were you?

SARAH: You should have let me.

ANNIE: It's all right.

SARAH: Well, we have to be off early. We won't be needing anything very much.

ANNIE: There isn't anything very much. Toast. Remains of the marmalade. Jam—damson, I think.

SARAH: That'll do us nicely.

ANNIE: Good. Well, it's all there. Help yourself.

SARAH: I suppose I'd better give Reg a call.

ANNIE: No, no. Don't overexert yourself. I'll do it.

SARAH: Thank you. He's in the sitting room I think. He should've brought down our suitcases.

ANNIE: Right.

[ANNIE *goes out.* SARAH *selects a piece of toast, examines it, finds it a little burnt and scrapes it distastefully. She sniffs the butter, finds it more or less okay. She sniffs the rather ancient-looking nearly-empty jar of marmalade. This she does reject. She sniffs the jam, decides that's all right and starts spreading her toast.* NORMAN *comes in.*]

NORMAN: Ah-ha. Breakfast. Good morning.

SARAH: [*not very warmly*] Good morning.

NORMAN. Sleep well?

SARAH: No.

NORMAN: I did.

SARAH: Good.

NORMAN: Are you angry with me?

SARAH: No.

NORMAN: This toast going free?

SARAH: Yes.

NORMAN: Cheer up, Sarah.

SARAH: And what is there to cheer me up? I have never been through such a shattering weekend in my life.

NORMAN: I'm sorry.

SARAH: It wasn't all your fault. Most of it was. But not entirely.

NORMAN: I think you ought to take care of yourself, you know.

SARAH: How do I do that?

NORMAN: Well. We don't want to lose you, do we?

SARAH: I don't think some people would mind one way or the other.

NORMAN: You find it hard to relax. That's the problem. I know that's your problem because it's my problem. As we were saying last night—I don't know how you keep going. I mean, I don't have two children and a house to run— and a husband. I've just got me. That's bad enough.

SARAH: I should imagine it would be.

NORMAN: But two children . . .

SARAH: You try explaining that to some people . . . Your wife for example.

NORMAN: Oh, well quite. She wouldn't understand.

SARAH: She doesn't.

NORMAN: I know as far as I'm concerned the whole thing's a miracle. Children. Just to think of the act of actually having them. Amazing. Damn it, Sarah, you've got something to be proud of, haven't you? If you look at it this way, just by having those kids of yours, you have been responsible for two miracles.

SARAH: Well, it's not that difficult.

NORMAN: It is to me. I've never done a miracle. I saw a film on it once. Childbirth. It came out as far as its ears and I fainted. Mind you, you wouldn't have been looking at it from the angle.

SARAH: I was unconscious. Both times.

NORMAN: Ah.

SARAH: It's afterwards, looking after them.

NORMAN: Quite.

SARAH: That's when it's difficult.

NORMAN: You must be exhausted. How old are they now?

SARAH: Denise is seven and Vincent's five.

NORMAN: Seven years you've been looking after children. Would it be impertinent to ask when you last had a holiday?

SARAH: I hoped this weekend was going to be one but—

NORMAN: No, be honest with me Sarah. When did you last have a holiday?

SARAH: I do not remember. It was too long ago.

NORMAN: Exactly. [*Pause*] You ought to get away. You need to. Can't you say to Reg, Reg I need a couple of days even. I must get away.

SARAH: He wouldn't take me away. And who's going to look after the children? It's no holiday with them. It was difficult enough this weekend. I was racing round organizing things, arranging this—

NORMAN: Go on your own. Leave him to look after them, for a change.

SARAH: Him?

NORMAN: Why not?

SARAH: Huh! [*Pause*] I wouldn't want to go on my own. What fun is it on your own?

[*Pause*.]

NORMAN: I'll take you if you like.

SARAH: I beg your pardon?

NORMAN: I said I'll take you.

SARAH: On holiday?

NORMAN: If you'd like to go.

SARAH: You must think I was born yesterday.

NORMAN: I would.

SARAH: You really have got a nerve.

NORMAN: I only offered. All right, all right . . .

SARAH: First Ruth, then Annie, then me.

NORMAN: Oh, Annie. That was different.

SARAH: How?

NORMAN: Well, it was. This would just be a holiday. For you. I'd take you round, give you a good weekend. Wouldn't you enjoy that?

SARAH: No.

NORMAN: Somewhere nice. What about Bournemouth? Ever been to Bournemouth?

SARAH: I have no desire to go to Bournemouth.

NORMAN: I've made you the offer. I leave it to you. Think about it. It would be above board. I'd book us a nice hotel. Breakfast in bed—separate breakfast. Separate beds. Separate rooms. Can't you imagine it? We'd wake up in the morning, side by side, in our separate rooms, and there's the sea. And we've got all day to look at it. No children to worry about. No husband to run after . . .

SARAH: Just you.

NORMAN: Just me. I'd like to see you happy, Sarah.

SARAH: Yes?

NORMAN: Yes. Is that wrong of me? To want to see you happy?

SARAH: Depends how you do it.

NORMAN: I'd give you a good time. We'd have fun. Have you ever been to Bournemouth? It's a great place. Laugh a minute.

SARAH: I can just see us going.

NORMAN: I'd very much like to make you happy.

SARAH: Pass the jam, would you?

NORMAN: Here.

[REG *enters*.]

REG: Ah, now where's the food?

SARAH: Where have you been?

REG: What do you mean, where have I been?

SARAH: Annie was supposed to call you ages ago.

REG: She did. I popped upstairs to Mother.

SARAH: What for?

REG: With the magazines. I took your magazines up to Mother. You told me to. Oh, Tom's here. Told you he'd come back, didn't I? Well, he's come back. I was looking out of the sitting room window and there he was, lurking in the garden. I told him I thought he was a cat burglar. [*He laughs*] I'm ravenous.

SARAH: Yes, all right. Well, just get yourself a piece of toast. We've got to go.

REG: What's the hurry?

SARAH: Because I want to get home early.

REG: What on earth for? The children aren't due back till this afternoon.

SARAH: And before that, I have to go over the house from top to bottom don't I? You may not realize it but the house has to be cleaned. It doesn't clean itself.

REG: You cleaned it before we left. Nobody's been in it since. How can it have got dirty?

SARAH: It's been standing for a whole weekend. Anyway, Mrs Bridges comes to clean tomorrow. I want to make sure it's clean before she does.

REG: Oh, I give up.

SARAH: You don't understand. You never will.

REG: Not much here to eat, is there?

SARAH: That's because there's nothing in the house.

REG: You're telling me. I've been starving since Saturday morning. On a diet of lettuce and soup.

SARAH: Now you know what it's like with nobody running after you, don't you?

REG: Oh, blimey, look at this toast, all cold and flabby. I can't eat this.

SARAH: Well, go and make some fresh.

REG: Where?

SARAH: In the greenhouse. Where do you think?

REG: All right, all right. You're in a really cheery mood this morning, aren't you?

[REG *goes out.*]

NORMAN: [*confidentially*] It's difficult isn't it? I know. Difficult sometimes . . . [*He pats her hand.*]

SARAH: Don't do that.

NORMAN: Why not?

SARAH: Because you're covering me in jam.

NORMAN: Sorry.

[*A pause.*]

SARAH: Were you just thinking about my health?

NORMAN: When?

SARAH: When you mentioned about this holiday? Did you want to take me away just for my health?

NORMAN: Well, that came into it. There might be any number of reasons. I'm easy. [*He smiles.*]

SARAH: So long as I know. [*She smiles.*]

[RUTH *enters.*]

RUTH: Norman.

NORMAN: Hallo.

RUTH: I'm ready.

NORMAN: Right. Want a spoonful of jam? That's all there is. Till Reg arrives with a blazing sliced loaf.

RUTH: I can wait.

NORMAN: Okay.

RUTH: Good morning, Sarah. [*No reply.*] Guess who isn't speaking to me this morning? I'll be in the sitting room, Norman, when you can tear yourself away from Mother Doom here.

NORMAN: Coming. [*He gets up, still eating.*]

[RUTH *goes out.*]

SARAH: Reg gets home about half-past six in the evening on weekdays.

NORMAN: Busy man.

SARAH: If you feel like giving me a ring any time. I'm usually tied to the house. I don't get out much.

NORMAN: I'd make you happy, Sarah.

SARAH: Yes.

NORMAN: Bye bye.

[NORMAN *goes out.* SARAH *looks thoughtful. She gives a pleased grunt.* REG *returns.*]

REG: Dear oh dear.

SARAH: Have you got it?

REG: What?

SARAH: I thought you were going to make yourself some toast.

REG: Oh, I don't know. I looked at the grill and I looked at the loaf and I thought—that's a lot of effort for a piece of toast. I'll make do with this piece.

SARAH: Well, I've finished.

REG: Tea's cold as well now. Not my day, is it?

SARAH: No, I don't think it is.

[ANNIE *and* TOM *enter.*]

ANNIE: Look who's here.

REG: I told you he was here.

TOM: Morning. Morning Sarah.

SARAH: Hallo Tom. Bright and early.

TOM: Yes. I didn't sleep very well, I'm afraid.

ANNIE: Just tea, Tom?

TOM: Just a cup, thank you.

REG: It's stone cold.

ANNIE: Well, I'll hot it up. That's easy enough.

[ANNIE *goes out with the teapot.*]

TOM: I wanted to apologize for last night.

SARAH: What?

TOM: Well—lashing out—Norman. Totally lost control. Feel very embarrassed about it.

SARAH: Nobody hurt fortunately.

TOM: No, I didn't get a very good swing. Bit rusty.

SARAH: Just as well.

TOM: Yes. Rather.

SARAH: I'm glad you've come back anyway.

TOM: I'm afraid I don't seem to be able to keep away.

SARAH: It'll be nice for Annie with us all going.

TOM: I'm only here for a second. I'm actually on my way to a call. Horse. Fetlock.

SARAH: Oh.

TOM: Not too serious. She can wait.

REG: Let her stand on three legs for a bit. [*He laughs.*]

TOM: No, she can stand all right.

SARAH: Well, I hope you'll look after Annie for us.

TOM: Oh yes, I'll do my best. I think she really looks after me. [*He laughs.*]

SARAH: Yes, well, you mustn't let it get too one-sided, must you?

TOM: What? Oh. No. I do help . . .

SARAH: Yes. It depends what you do though, doesn't it?

TOM: I did the ceiling in the kitchen. And—

SARAH: No, I meant a little more than that.

REG: I thought we were in a hurry.

SARAH: Oh. Yes.

REG: Will we see you at Christmas, Tom? Or are you going to Scotland again?

TOM: Probably.

REG: Oh, well. Sometime. All the best.

[ANNIE *enters with the teapot.*]

ANNIE: Are you off?

SARAH: Yes, we must.

ANNIE: Okay, I'll come and see you've got everything. Here you are, Tom. I topped it up.

TOM: Thanks.

ANNIE: Be back in a sec.

REG: Bye.

SARAH: Goodbye, Tom.

TOM: Bye.

[SARAH, ANNIE *and* REG *go out.* TOM *sits alone. He pours the tea. It is practically white.*]

Oh. Oh well . . .

[*He sits and sings to himself.* TOM *on his own is amazingly cheerful. He amuses himself by arranging the things on the table in a strange secret pattern of his own. At length,* ANNIE *returns.*]

ANNIE: All right?

TOM: Fine. All gone have they?

ANNIE: Just about. Norman and Ruth seem to be having trouble starting their car.

TOM: Oh, should I . . .? [*He half rises.*]

ANNIE: No. Enjoy your tea.

TOM: Oh yes.

ANNIE: Have you got any tea in there or is it just milk?

TOM: No, it is tea. Bit anaemic.

ANNIE: I'll make some more in a minute. Quite a week-end.

TOM: Yes.

ANNIE: I've behaved very badly. I'm sorry.

TOM: No. It's me—

ANNIE: No. [*Pause.*] Tom . . .

TOM: Um?

ANNIE: Has your—opinion of me gone down as a result of this weekend? I mean, do you think less of me?

TOM: Good Lord, no.

ANNIE: You still—like me?

TOM: Oh yes. Of course I do.

ANNIE: You'll still come round?

TOM: You bet. [*He laughs*] Once you've improved the tea, anyway.

ANNIE: The only reason I said I would go with Norman, you see, was—I suddenly felt very lonely.

TOM: Yes, I understand. It's all right. We all get lonely. If you're lonely again and I'm not here, why don't you give me a ring?

ANNIE: This is a very big house you see. Most of the time it's just Mother and me here. We'll have to sell it eventually, it's ridiculous.

TOM: I wouldn't do that.

ANNIE: We'll have to. We'll have to move somewhere smaller. Perhaps in Essex. Or Norfolk. Or Northumberland.

TOM: Bit off the beaten track.

ANNIE: Yes.

TOM: Wouldn't see much of me.

ANNIE: No.

TOM: Well, if you do sell it, make sure you give me first refusal, won't you? [*He gets up.*] Well, I'd better go and see to my horse.

ANNIE: Yes. Go and see to your horse.

[ANNIE *turns the sideplate in front of her upside down on the table. She bangs on it deliberately with a spoon. A regular sort of rhythm which, although not fast, grows in intensity until the plate breaks.*]

TOM: [*watching her curiously*] What on earth are you doing?

ANNIE: Breaking things. Breaking things for breakfast.

TOM: [*laughs awkwardly*] Careful of splinters.

[NORMAN *rushes in in mac and hat.*]

NORMAN: Disaster! We cannot start it.

TOM: Oh goodness. Want a hand?

NORMAN: Need one of these ex-boxers to give it a shove.

TOM: Right. My pleasure. Probably see you later, Annie.

ANNIE: Yes.

[TOM *goes.* NORMAN *is about to follow. He notices* ANNIE *and the plate.*]

NORMAN: What are you doing? Don't tell me, you've finally run out of food. I told you you'd get round to eating the plates eventually. Now the nicest way to eat a plate—is spread it with a thin layer of jam and then pour custard all over the—

[ANNIE *flies at* NORMAN *and clings on to him.*]

ANNIE: Oh Norman . . .

NORMAN: Only you want to make sure it's thick custard.

ANNIE: [*muffled*] I want—

NORMAN: Eh?

ANNIE: I want . . .

NORMAN: I can't hear you. What?

ANNIE: [*a wail*] I want to go to East Grinstead.

NORMAN: [*soothing her*] All right. Fine. I'll take you. I'll take you.

ANNIE: [*tearfully*] Will you?

NORMAN: Just say the word. Come on now, don't cry. I'll make you happy. Don't worry. I'll make you happy.
[*He hugs her to him.* ANNIE *clings on.* NORMAN *smiles happily.*]

Curtain

LIVING TOGETHER

Characters

REG
SARAH, his wife
RUTH, Reg's sister
NORMAN, her husband
ANNIE, Reg and Ruth's younger sister
TOM

Scene: The Sitting Room

Time: A weekend in July

ACT ONE

Scene One

The sitting room. Saturday 6.30 p.m. A high ceilinged Victorian room in need of redecoration. Doors leading to the garden and another to the rest of the house. Furnishings include a settee, easy chairs, a small table, an occasional table and a fireplace in front of which is a brown fur rug.

SARAH, dressed in her light summer coat and dress, is in the process of lifting a suitcase from the floor onto the table to open it.

REG enters from the garden in cap and sports jacket carrying one more bag. He is followed by NORMAN, bearded, in woolly hat and raincoat, carrying his own battered suitcase. He flings himself down into a chair and sits grumpily. REG takes his bag to SARAH.

REG: That's the lot. Well, come on. Where is she then? Where is she? Where's my little sister?

SARAH: Ssh. Mother's resting.

REG: Oh. [*Wandering back to the window*] We ought to cut down the vegetation in the tennis court and have a game, Norman. Fancy a game?

NORMAN: I hate tennis.

SARAH: I thought you were in a hurry to go somewhere, Norman.

NORMAN: Not at all.

REG: Yes, I thought you said you had a—librarian's conference.

NORMAN: It's been cancelled.

REG: When?

NORMAN: About ten seconds ago. Due to lack of interest.

REG: Funny lot these librarians. Now, where's Annie, do you know?

SARAH: She's in there.

REG: Ah. [*He moves to the door.*]

SARAH: Wait.

REG: Why?

SARAH: She's busy. Tom's in there with her, having a talk.

REG: Well, she can talk to Tom any time. I've come all the way to see her.

SARAH: Wait.

REG: What made her change her mind? About going? I mean, I thought the idea was, we came down here, nursed Mother for the weekend and Annie went off somewhere and had a good time. No point in us being here now, is there? Might as well not have come. Not that I mind. Nice to see the country. Beautiful evening. No kids . . .

SARAH: Where did you pack that present for Mother?

REG: What present?

SARAH: The bed jacket. The blue bed jacket, it was wrapped in tissue. Where is it?

REG: Never set eyes on it.

SARAH: [*removing a large playing board, bits of cardboard etc. from the case*] What's all this you've packed?

REG: My game.

SARAH: Why did you want to bring it down here?

REG: I thought there might be someone around, we could try it out. I've invented it, I want to try it out. I mean, the kids won't play it with me, you won't play it with me —how do I know if it works if no one'll play it? Norman can play.

NORMAN: Eh?

SARAH: I should think Norman's had enough of games, haven't you Norman?

REG: Eh?

SARAH: Anyway, Norman's going in a minute, aren't you Norman?

REG: What's all this? What's going on between you two?

SARAH: I'll tell you later.

REG: Oh, yes . . .? If you're planning an affair, let me know and I'll book my holiday.

SARAH: [*giving up her search*] Oh well, that's that. No present for Mother. You've forgotten to pack it. [*Picking up a carrier bag and removing a bundle of women's magazines*] Oh well, I'll give her these magazines and tell her we'll send the bed jacket on to her. It took me ages to make that. If you knew how I hated knitting.

REG: We do. We know. We sat round all winter watching her with bated breath. One dropped stitch and you could say goodbye to your supper . . . Hey, one of my little men is missing.

SARAH: Oh, my God.

REG: I've lost my Chief Superintendent. Is he at the bottom of the suitcase?

SARAH: I have no idea. Our house is littered with little men.

REG: And she's complaining. [*He chuckles.*]

SARAH: You've very pensive, Norman.

NORMAN: I'm wondering which is the cleanest and quickest way to finish myself off.

REG: Well, don't get married. That's long and messy. Ah-ha, here he is. [*He holds up a small cardboard figure on a base which he has rescued from the suitcase*] The Chief Superintendent in person. Nearly had a nasty accident. Got himself tangled up in a nasty web of blue woolly . . . oh.

SARAH: Give that to me. [*She retrieves her bedjacket from* REG.]

REG: It was there all the time. Just needed a good copper to find it.

SARAH: Would you mind taking these upstairs?

REG: [*taking the suitcases*] My pleasure. [*He moves to the door, whistling.*]

SARAH: And don't wake Mother if she's dozing.

REG: I'll go and say hallo to Annie first.

SARAH: I've told you, she's—

REG: I haven't seen her for three months. She's my sister. I want to say hallo.

SARAH: She and Tom are—

REG: Oh, to blazes with Tom.
  [REG *goes out whistling.*]

SARAH: [*turning her attention to* NORMAN] It's no good sitting there looking sorry for yourself. I'm appalled at you, I really am.

NORMAN: [*leering*] Jealous?

SARAH: Don't be disgusting. Annie of all people. How could you? What on earth made you do it?

NORMAN: I haven't done anything.

SARAH: Annie has told me everything.

NORMAN: Has she? And what could she possibly tell you?

SARAH: About you two—last Christmas. In this house. With your wife ill upstairs—rolling about with her sister on this very rug.

NORMAN: Oh—that . . . that was just festive fun.

SARAH: And if that isn't enough, planning to sneak off with her for some sordid weekend.

NORMAN: There's nothing sordid about East Grinstead. She wanted to come. I wanted to go. Don't you see? It would have been something different for her—exciting. And for me. She's stuck here, all on her own, day after day looking after that old sabre-toothed bat upstairs . . .

SARAH: Will you not refer to Mother like that.

NORMAN: Oh, come on. She's not your Mother, she's not my Mother. She's a mother-in-law. Fair game. I'll call her what I like. You ought to hear what Annie calls her sometimes . . . Anyway, we happen to love each other. Me and Annie that is, not me and mother-in-law.

SARAH: Don't be ridiculous. You're married to Ruth.

NORMAN: What's that got to do with it?

SARAH: And Annie, I may remind you, has her fiancé to consider.

NORMAN: [*scornful*] Her who?

SARAH: Her—well—her whatever she calls him—Tom.

NORMAN: Tom.

SARAH: Yes. He may not be ideal in many ways but beggars can't be choosers—

NORMAN: She's not a beggar.

SARAH: Maybe not. But it would be stupid to make out she

had a very wide choice as regards a possible husband. She's not—well . . .

NORMAN: She's beautiful.

SARAH: I'm not going to argue. Certainly no-one could describe her as beautiful. I'll admit she has a great deal of—

NORMAN: Anybody I love is automatically beautiful.

SARAH: Oh, Norman, don't be ridiculous.

NORMAN: Have you never felt that way? Perhaps you've never been in love. Maybe that's your trouble. Was Reg never beautiful in your eyes?

SARAH: I'm not discussing my private life . . .

NORMAN: You're being free enough with mine, aren't you?

SARAH: Yours doesn't happen to be particularly private, does it? It happens to involve about half a dozen people. You, Annie, Ruth, Tom, Reg, me and Mother.

NORMAN: I've never asked Mother for a weekend any-where. [*Moving to window*] Look at that cat up there. He's still up that tree. Tom was trying to get it down. He can't be much of a vet. What sort of a vet are you, when you terrify your patients into climbing trees? Something wrong with his basket-side manner, I'd say. What do you say, Sarah? Would you say you were a fulfilled person?

SARAH: I don't know what you mean.

NORMAN: Are you happy then?

SARAH: Yes—mostly. Occasionally. Now and then. I don't know. I don't have time to think about it. When you've a family like mine you're too busy—

NORMAN: You're very lucky. I can't say Ruth and I are happy.

SARAH: Well, I'm not surprised if you— [*Checking herself*] She's not the easiest person I admit.

NORMAN: No.

SARAH: Then neither are you.

NORMAN: I'm very warm and affectionate, you know.

SARAH: Yes. So are dogs. But they don't make particularly good husbands.

NORMAN: Ah well, like me, they invariably marry—lady dogs. Perhaps I should leave her.

SARAH: Yes, do. Please do. I think it would be better for both of you. But for heaven's sake, clear off completely and whatever you do, stop pestering Annie. She doesn't want you, not really.

NORMAN: I supposed you talked her out of going away with me.

SARAH: I didn't need to. She'd already made up her own mind. I certainly didn't encourage her . . . I must go up and see Mother.

NORMAN: It was going to be a lovely time. We were going to meet behind the Post Office in the village at seven o'clock and steal away on the bus to our hotel. Forget everything, everybody, just lie anonymously in each other's arms. Just for a day.

SARAH: We'd still be here when you came back.

NORMAN: I feel terribly depressed.

SARAH: Serve you right.

NORMAN: You haven't told Tom, have you?

SARAH: That's up to Annie. Nothing to do with me.

NORMAN: Nothing? You only talked her out of going.

SARAH: I have already said, I did no such thing. It was Annie's decision.

NORMAN: I hope she doesn't tell Tom.

SARAH: Why?

NORMAN: It'd upset him.

SARAH: It's a bit late to consider his feelings now, isn't it? Having tried to steal Annie from under his nose.

NORMAN: I wasn't stealing her, I was borrowing her. For the weekend.

SARAH: Make her sound like one of your library books.

NORMAN: She was borrowing me too. It was mutual. It was a friendly loan. We never intended to upset anybody. We both agreed. That was the joy of it, don't you see? Nobody need ever have known. If Annie hadn't gone and told you . . . nobody.

SARAH: Oh, well. It's up to Annie if she wants to tell Tom. Nothing to do with me. [*She tries to lift the magazine pile*] Oh, these are far too heavy, I'll get Reg to take them up later. Now for goodness sake, Norman, pull yourself together and go home to Ruth. [*Examining bed jacket*] Look how he's creased this, honestly, after the trouble I took to iron it.

NORMAN: Why did you stop her going, Sarah? Be honest. Why?

SARAH: I've told you why . . .

[SARAH *goes out.*]

NORMAN: [*mournfully*] I really am very depressed.

[*He mooches about. He pulls a magazine from the pile and flips through it. Something catches his eye and he starts reading. After a moment, he starts to laugh. He finds the article increasingly hysterical.* ANNIE *comes in. She stares at him.*]

ANNIE: Norman.

NORMAN: [*springing up guiltily*] Oh. Hallo, Annie.

ANNIE: You all right?

NORMAN: Yes, I was just trying to cheer myself up.

ANNIE: Looks like you've succeeded.

NORMAN: No.

ANNIE: Norman, I'm awfully sorry. Really. I expect Sarah's told you.

NORMAN: She said you'd—thought better of it.

ANNIE: Yes. I feel dreadful after all the trouble you've taken. Booking East Grinstead and things. It's just . . .

NORMAN: It's all right. [*Pause*] Oh, why did you let her talk you out of it?

ANNIE: I didn't.

NORMAN: Don't tell me you'd have changed your mind if she hadn't . . .

ANNIE: Things were getting very complicated, you see. I mean, when we were planning it, last Christmas and on the phone and things—well—it was simple then, wasn't it? It was easy just to forget about Ruth and—Tom and so on. Not that Tom's all that important but after all, you are married to Ruth and she is my sister, even if I'm not all that fond of her but I don't think I'm very good at pretending for very long. Sarah got it out of me in no time.

NORMAN: Yes. She would.

ANNIE: And I don't think I'd have been much fun to be with, anyway. I'd have been worrying all the time. Are you furious with me?

NORMAN: No.

ANNIE: Oh Norman, you look so miserable. I am sorry.

NORMAN: Don't . . .

ANNIE: What?

NORMAN: Don't kneel on that rug if you don't mind. It reminds me.

ANNIE: Oh yes. Our rug. [*A short giggle*] I got the fire tongs mended.

NORMAN: Oh yes.

ANNIE: Tom fixed them.

NORMAN: Oh. What does he have to say about all this?

ANNIE: Tom? I don't think he knows.

NORMAN: He doesn't?

ANNIE: I haven't told him.

NORMAN: Oh.

ANNIE: Sarah might.

NORMAN: I bet she will. She said she won't. But she will. She'll be dropping big circular hints. She's never kept a secret in her life . . .

ANNIE: She'll have to chalk it up in huge letters. You know, I'm really very fond of Tom but he really is terribly heavy going. Like running up hill in roller skates. Not like you. "Beautiful sunset, isn't it Tom?" "Um." Everything's um. Probably works a treat when he's stamping out swine fever but it's pretty boring over dinner. "Do you like the wine, Tom?" "Um." Honestly. Norman?

NORMAN: Mmm? I mean, yes.

ANNIE: What are you going to tell Ruth?

NORMAN: What I was going to tell her anyway. I've been on a conference.

ANNIE: Which finished early?

NORMAN: Something like that. We ran out of things to talk about. What does it matter? She won't care. She probably thinks I'm in the attic mending the roof.

ANNIE: I didn't know Assistant Librarians had conferences.

NORMAN: Everybody has conferences.

ANNIE: You'll be able to get back all right?

NORMAN: Yes.

ANNIE: Oh dear . . .

NORMAN: What?

ANNIE: You look so limp. Like an old tea towel.

[ANNIE *impulsively leans forward to kiss him on the cheek.* REG *enters.*]

NORMAN: [*seeing him*] Look out.

[ANNIE *jumps away.*]

REG: [*standing awkwardly*] Er—hallo again. Excuse me, just came in for something. [*He stands uncertainly.*]

NORMAN: What?

REG: What? Yes—what?—er. [*He picks up the wastepaper basket.*] Ah. This is it. This is it. Thank you. Carry on. [REG *goes out.*]

NORMAN: Do you ever get the feeling you're being watched? Sarah's secret agent. Our days together are numbered.

ANNIE: So are our minutes.

NORMAN: [*rising and going to the window*] Come on then.

ANNIE: What?

NORMAN: It's now or never. What do you say?

ANNIE: What is?

NORMAN: We can be through the gap in the hedge and halfway down the lane before they realize we've gone.

ANNIE: [*drawing back*] Oh, Norman . . .

NORMAN: What's to stop us? I love you—you love me— we're in love. We should be together. It's right. Believe me, it's right. We have right on our side.

ANNIE: [*doubtfully*] Well . . .

NORMAN: Don't you see, we're not alone? We've got the

whole tradition of history behind us. We're not the first lovers who've ever done this—stood up to the whole establishment and said to hell with the status quo, we don't care what's meant to be, we mean this to be. Us. And there's nothing can stand in our way, you know. Not if you think about it. What is there to stop us?

ANNIE: Mother's pills . . .

NORMAN: Eh?

ANNIE: I can't just rush away. I have to explain to them about Mother's pills.

NORMAN: [*passionately*] My God! The course of true love shattered, not by the furies, not by the fates but by Mother's bleeding pills.

ANNIE: Not only that.

NORMAN: It's all right. That's enough to be getting on with. Don't swamp me with any more overwhelming arguments. Dear Juliet, my shoelace has come undone, I cannot join you in the tomb, Love, Romeo. Dear Tristan, Owing to a sudden tax demand . . .

ANNIE: All right, Norman, all right,

[*Pause.* NORMAN *simmers down.*]

NORMAN: That's it then.

ANNIE: Yes. That's it.

NORMAN: Oh.

[*A pause.* TOM *enters.*]

TOM: Ah.

NORMAN: Gone. All gone.

TOM: Glad I've caught you.

NORMAN: Oh, it's Tom. Hallo, Tom. Haven't seen you for ages. How are you?

TOM: Fine. Just been talking to you in the garden, haven't I?

NORMAN: Oh yes. I forgot. I think it was me.

TOM: Don't quite follow you.

NORMAN: It was probably me. On the other hand it could have been you.

TOM: Me what?

NORMAN: Talking to yourself.

ANNIE: Norman ...

TOM: Hang on, I'm getting confused here.

NORMAN: How unusual.

ANNIE: Norman ...

NORMAN: [*sitting*] Anyway, my mistake.

TOM: [*doubtful*] Yes. I—wanted a word with you.

ANNIE: [*moving to door*] I'll get on out there.

TOM: No. Hang on. Hang on a second, Annie. Would you mind?

NORMAN: Recriminations. Here they come ...

TOM: Um?

NORMAN: Nothing.

TOM: The point is ... [*He pauses uncertainly and wanders to the window*] Is that cat still up that tree, by the way?

NORMAN: Hanging on grimly. As we all are.

TOM: I suppose he'll come down eventually ... The point is, something seems to be going on which I'm not being let into.

NORMAN: Has it?

TOM: Apparently. Sarah was talking about something ...

NORMAN: [*to* ANNIE] What did I tell you?

TOM: What?

NORMAN: Come on, let's have it. What did she say?

TOM: That's it, you see. I couldn't make it out.

NORMAN: You couldn't?

TOM: Not really.

NORMAN: Oh—good.

ANNIE: Would you both like something to drink?

TOM: Thought perhaps you could enlighten me.

NORMAN: Yes, please. A great deal.

ANNIE: I'll see what we've got.

[ANNIE *goes out.*]

TOM: Annie's a bit angry with me.

NORMAN: Is she?

TOM: Yes. You know she was planning to go away this weekend.

NORMAN: Yes.

TOM: Well, reading between the lines, I think she was rather hoping that old you-know-who would go with her.

NORMAN: Who?

TOM: Me.

NORMAN: You?

TOM: Yes.

NORMAN: She asked you?

TOM: Very obliquely.

NORMAN: Must have been.

TOM: Now she's not going. And it seems to be my fault.

NORMAN: It is.

TOM: You think so?

NORMAN: Definitely. If she's not going away, it's entirely due to you.

TOM: Yes, I was afraid of that. The question is, how do I get myself out of the dog's kennel and back in the pantry?

NORMAN: I beg your pardon?

TOM: Back in her good books.

NORMAN: Very difficult.

TOM: Is it?

NORMAN: Want my opinion?

TOM: I'd welcome it.

NORMAN: I think you've given her too much. I think she's in danger of being spoilt. She's taking you for granted.

TOM: Really?

NORMAN: She's taking everyone for granted. What she needs is a bit of the old boot.

TOM: Boot?

NORMAN: Bit of the rough stuff.

TOM: Oh, come on. Boot? Come on . . .

NORMAN: Metaphorical.

TOM: Oh, metaphorical boot. What's that exactly?

NORMAN: Tell her she's damned lucky to have you around. And the next time she's planning holidays for two, she can come and ask you politely if you'd like to come. If you don't watch it, she'll walk all over you. Couple of sharp

words, she'll jump. Tell her she looks a mess. If she
wants to be seen around with you in future, she'd better
smarten up her ideas. She looks like something that's
fallen off a Post van. I mean, what the hell right has
she to promise something and then let you down at the
last minute? It would serve her right if you belted her
one and gave her rabies. That's my opinion. [*He pauses
breathless.*]

TOM: [*very bewildered*] Is it?

NORMAN: She'd respect you for that.

TOM: Well, I'll bear it in mind but . . .

[ANNIE *returns with a tray of glasses and four bottles of home
made wine tucked under her arms. She is having difficulty.*]

ANNIE: It'll have to be the home made stuff.

TOM: [*leaping up*] Oh, let me . . . [*He takes a bottle which
appears to be slipping from under her arm.*]

ANNIE: Thanks.

[TOM *catches* NORMAN's *eye.* NORMAN *shakes his head disapprovingly.* TOM *stares at the bottle he is holding.* ANNIE
stands waiting for TOM *to take the other bottles from her.
Instead,* TOM *puts his bottle back on her tray and sits.*]

Oh thank you so much. That's a great help. Don't put
yourselves out, will you?

NORMAN: No.

TOM: No.

ANNIE: What's got into you two?

NORMAN: Nothing.

TOM: No.

ANNIE: Well, if you want a drink, you can damn well open
them.

[*She throws the bottle opener to* TOM, *who catches it, hesitates and
finally gets up.* NORMAN *clucks disapprovingly.*]

TOM: Well . . . parsnip or dandelion?

NORMAN: We have a choice?

TOM: Both last year's. I think I'd recommend the parsnip.
It's slightly mellower. The dandelion's rather lethal. Oh
and there's some carrot.

ANNIE: Don't touch the dandelion—it's a killer. I didn't mean to bring it in.

TOM: Parsnip then?

NORMAN: Dandelion.

TOM: You sure?

NORMAN: Positive.

TOM: Oh well . . . [*He starts to open bottles.*]

ANNIE: I have a feeling there's trouble brewing in the dining room. I passed the door just now and Reg and Sarah seemed to be limbering up.

NORMAN: That should set the seal on the weekend.

ANNIE: As long as Mother doesn't hear them.

TOM: No, we don't want her upset.

ANNIE: It won't upset her. She'll insist on being carried downstairs to be in at the kill. There's nothing she likes better than a good row.

NORMAN: In the old days, she used to start them all.

ANNIE: She and Sarah. She really loathed Sarah.

NORMAN: She's not all bad.

ANNIE: Tom's frightened to go up there, aren't you?

TOM: Well . . .

ANNIE: She thinks he's a doctor.

TOM: Can't get it through to her I'm a vet. She insists I take her pulse, listen to her—chest and other things. Very embarrassing.

NORMAN: She's mad for the feel of manly hands. She knows what she's doing, don't worry.

TOM: Yes, I think she does. [*Examining a glassful of wine*] Better just try this first. [*He samples it.*]

ANNIE: [*loudly in* NORMAN'*s direction*] What's it like, Tom?

TOM: Um? . . . [*He ponders.*]

ANNIE: [*raising her eyebrows to heaven, softly*] Um . . .

TOM: [*bringing the glasses to them*] Not bad, not bad, here . . .

ANNIE: Thanks.

NORMAN: Ta.

ANNIE: [*examining her glass*] It's clearer than usual.

TOM: Yes.

ANNIE: It's usually like soup. You have to filter it through your front teeth.

NORMAN: [*raising his glass by way of a toast*] Well. Um . . .

ANNIE: [*giggling*] Um . . .

TOM: Yes. Cheers. [*Pause*] Um . . . you know, I've been thinking. What would have been rather nice. Too late now—but another year. Supposing there is another year that is . . .

NORMAN: Why? Are you planning to bring the world to an end shortly?

TOM: No, no.

NORMAN: This is very potent.

ANNIE: Very. Brewed by Mother. Last thing she did before she was ill.

NORMAN: She knows her spells.

TOM: What would have been rather nice . . .

NORMAN: [*finding a bit in his glass*] Ah.

ANNIE: What is it?

NORMAN: Bit of cork. Or a toad's leg.

TOM: What would have been awfully nice is if we'd all three gone. Don't you think?

[ANNIE *and* NORMAN *stare at him.*]

I mean, we all get on well. It would have been rather fun . . .

NORMAN: I beg your pardon?

TOM: If Annie and you and I had all gone away together on her weekend.

NORMAN: [*highly amused*] Oh, my God. [*Rising and crossing to the wine*] More wine . . .

TOM: Single rooms, of course.

NORMAN: [*taking up the bottle of dandelion wine and returning to his chair*] Oh yes, single rooms.

TOM: I didn't mean anything like that.

NORMAN: [*laughing openly*] No. Nothing like that.

TOM: What's funny?

NORMAN: [*helpless*] Nothing.

ANNIE: [*angry*] Oh Tom, honestly.

TOM: Eh?

ANNIE: You're so dim. You're so completely and utterly dismally dim.

TOM: What?

ANNIE: You make me mad, you're so stupid. You're boring, slow-witted, dull and utterly stupid.

TOM: [*slightly injured, no more*] What have I said now? What have I said now?

NORMAN: Now's the time to knock her down.

ANNIE: I'm fed up with both of you. You've ruined my weekend.

TOM: All I said was—

ANNIE: [*yelling*] I heard what you said. Thank you very much. I heard what you said.

[NORMAN *is still laughing, highly amused by this.*]

And Norman, just shut up.

[NORMAN *does so. A silence.*]

TOM: Well . . .

ANNIE: [*muttering*] Stupid men . . .

[*A crash from the dining room.*]

NORMAN: Meanwhile, in the dining room, the first shots are being fired in anger.

ANNIE: [*leaping up*] Oh, no . . . [*hurrying to the door*] I wish you'd all go away, all of you, and leave me in peace.

[ANNIE *goes out.*]

TOM: She's like a tiger when she's roused, isn't she?

NORMAN: I've never met a tiger socially, I wouldn't know.

TOM: Something's got into her, you know. I think that holiday meant more to her than she's letting on.

NORMAN: Yes, I'm beginning to think that. [*Proffering bottle*] Another one?

TOM: No, no. Spoil my dinner. You'd better be careful or you'll finish up here for the night.

NORMAN: That's a point. [*He pours himself another.*]

[TOM *moves to the window.*]

TOM: [*calling*] Pussy, pussy. Down puss. Come down, puss. Pussy, pussy. I wish they'd given the animal a name. I really do. [NORMAN *pours another glass*] I should go easy on that. I had a very unpleasant side reaction.

NORMAN: It doesn't show.

TOM: Well, I think I'll go and see if I can pour oil on things. Not going immediately, are you?

NORMAN: Not immediately.

TOM: Right.

[TOM *goes out.* NORMAN *rises to his feet and finds already he's a bit unsteady. He goes to the table and collects the bottle of parsnip wine.*]

NORMAN: [*on his way back via the window, calling*] You stay up there, mate. If you come down, he'll only want paying. [TOM *returns.*]

TOM: Oh, Lord . . .

NORMAN: Back again?

TOM: I think I'll keep out of there for a second. The room's positively knee-deep in home truths—if you know what I mean.

NORMAN: Splendid.

TOM: That and biscuits.

NORMAN: Biscuits?

TOM: Yes, they seem to have been throwing biscuits around. Water biscuits.

NORMAN: You can do someone a nasty injury with a water biscuit . . . [ANNIE *appears fleetingly in the doorway with a dustpan and brush.*]

ANNIE: All hell's been let loose in there.

[ANNIE *goes.*]

TOM: Do you need a . . . [*He realizes she's gone.*]

[*Pause.* TOM *wanders to the table and discovers* REG's *game. Examining it*] What's all this? Looks like another of Reg's home-made games. Looks even more complicated than usual. I better keep out of the way if he decides to play it. Reg gets rather irritated with me. Always very slow on getting the hang of the rules. [*Slight pause*] Norman. Frankly—answer me something.

NORMAN: Mmm?

TOM: Do you think I'm dim and dismal? I think that's what she said. Yes, that was it. Dim and dismal and stupid. Do I come across as that?

NORMAN: No. I'd say—you had the good fortune to be born without a single suspicious or malicious thought in your head.

TOM: Oh, I don't know.

NORMAN: Yes. Yes, true. And that can get you in a lot of trouble. Because you're more or less on your own, you see. And whenever people feel like taking a really good swing at something to relieve their feelings, you come in extremely handy. No comeback, you see.

TOM: I haven't noticed people doing that. You've got the wrong chap.

NORMAN: [*waving a fist in the air*] You've got to develop a comeback. [*Studying* TOM] I mean, looking at you standing there, I don't think there's anyone in there at all. You're somewhere else. That's remote control, all that lot.

TOM: That stuff's beginning to tell. I warned you about the dandelion.

NORMAN: Don't worry about a thing.

TOM: Well I'd better go and see if the dining room's cooled off a bit. I'll take them in a bottle. [*He takes one.*]

NORMAN: Want a tip?

TOM: What?

NORMAN: Go in there laughing.

TOM: Laughing?

NORMAN: There's nothing they like better in this family than a good laugh. Go on. Bring an atmosphere of merriment into the room.

TOM: All right. I'll try it. You're a good chap, Norman, you know. A very good chap.

NORMAN: Thank you.

TOM: I'm sorry you're having to dash away. To your—

conference. Pity you're not staying. You brighten the place up a bit. Pity. Cheerio.

NORMAN: Cheerio.

[TOM *goes out.* NORMAN, *left alone, rises, kicks off his shoes and for the first time takes off his coat. He rolls down onto the hearthrug and lies on his back.*]

Here's to you, Tom old buddy. Here's to the lot of you.

[*He starts to sing softly, then louder.*]

Curtain

ACT ONE

SCENE TWO

The sitting room. Saturday 8 p.m. NORMAN *is now asleep, rolled up in the rug. Beside him, bottles and a glass.* REG *and* TOM *enter without seeing him.*

REG: . . . no, no. You say to me, who's there, you see . . .

TOM: Oh, it's me who says that. I see. All right. Who's there?

REG: Start again. Knock knock.

TOM: Come in—I mean, who's there?

REG: Vet.

TOM: Vet?

REG: No. You say, vet who?

TOM: Vet who, sorry. Come in—who's there—vet who?

REG: There's no "come in". Start again.

TOM: Right ho. Knock knock.

REG: Who's there . . . no. I should have started it. Knock knock.

TOM: Who's there?

REG: Vet.

TOM: Vet who?

REG: Vet kind of door is this, you can't afford a bell? [*He laughs.*]

TOM: Yes, I think I've got it now—try it again.

REG: That's it.

TOM: Oh, is it? Quite simple really.

REG: Yes . . . [*Seeing* NORMAN] Good God! Look at that.

TOM: Oh. It's Norman. [*They move to him.*] Is he all right?

REG: Norman! Norman! [*No response.*] He's out like a light.

TOM: I thought he'd gone.

REG: So did everybody. When he finally stopped singing and peace descended over the fruit and cream, I thought we'd lost him. Sarah's going to be pleased.

TOM: Ought we to move him?

REG: Well, he's not in anybody's way. Oy— [*He kicks* NORMAN.]

[NORMAN *grunts.*]

[*Moving away*] Leave him, I think. Oh, I'm starving after that meal. Salad. I can't bear salad. It grows while you're eating it, you know. Have you noticed? You start one side of your plate and by the time you've got to the other, there's a fresh crop of lettuce taken root and sprouted up. You have to start again. And it still doesn't fill you. You finish up exhausted and hungry.

TOM: [*still with* NORMAN] He's still breathing.

REG: I should hope so. He's enough trouble as he is without dying on us. The problem with this house is there's no television.

TOM: It's very shallow breathing. Do you think I should take his hat off?

REG: He doesn't breathe through the top of his head, does he? Or I don't know, he might do, knowing Norman. [*Bending over him*] If I were you, I'd pull it down over his face—like this. [*He does so*] There you are, great improvement.

TOM: It's the dandelion, you see. Look at that, he's had nearly a bottle. Drowning his sorrows, I suspect.

REG: Sorrows?

TOM: Well, I was talking to him earlier. He was obviously very disturbed. Depressed . . .

REG: Was he? Well . . .

TOM: Don't know why, I'm sure. You know something, though, I've got a theory there's probably a woman at the back of it. Man gets drunk like this, it's generally a woman. Ruth, do you think?

REG: Possibly. Possibly . . .

TOM: Perhaps Sarah would know. She usually keeps her ear close to the ground. Better ask her.

REG: [*hastily*] No I wouldn't, Tom, really.

TOM: No?

REG: No. The point is, Sarah did whisper something to me, as a matter of fact. Norman mentioned something to her. Confidentially.

TOM: Oh. Did he? Anything we can do to help? I mean, he's a good chap. Pity to see him like this.

REG: Well apparently, he had something lined up for to-night, you see.

TOM: Yes, his Annual Librarian's Conference. He told me. He'll have missed that now, won't he?

REG: No, it was something else, you see. He'd apparently lined up a bit on the side.

TOM: A bit on the side?

REG: Oh, you know Norman. Any pretty girl . . . he's away.

TOM: Oh, I see. And she's let him down?

REG: Apparently.

TOM: I see. Any idea who she is?

REG: No. No. None at all.

TOM: Oh. Pity. I mean, it might have been worth almost trying to contact her. Seeing if we couldn't patch things up. Mind you, if she could see him now, she'd probably feel she'd made the right decision.

[ANNIE *comes in.*]

ANNIE: I have never known a house where you can have a blazing row over who's going to make the coffee . . . [*Seeing* NORMAN] Oh, no! Norman! What's the matter with him?

REG: He's taken an overdose.

ANNIE: An overdose? Of what? [*Trying to revive* NORMAN] Norman . . . Norman.

TOM: Of dandelion wine.

ANNIE: What?

TOM: He's had too much of it, that's all.

ANNIE: You mean, he's just drunk?

REG: Give her a prize.

ANNIE: Norman, you idiot—get up— [*She kicks him.*]

NORMAN: [*sleepily*] Hallo.

ANNIE: Oh, look at him, he's disgusting. Sarah'll be delighted to see him. I thought he'd gone home.

TOM: No, well—actually—we were just saying, he's probably like this because of his bit on the side.

ANNIE: Bit on the side?

REG: Yes, well, we don't want to go into all that now, Tom.

ANNIE: What bit on the side?

TOM: Oh, you know Norman. Any pretty girl. He'd got some bit on the side lined up for the weekend. She went and ditched him.

ANNIE: Norman told you that?

REG: No.

TOM: You've just said he did.

REG: Yes, well he did but . . .

TOM: Yes, he did.

ANNIE: He did? [*Kicking* NORMAN] Get up, you drunken slob.

NORMAN: Hallo.

REG: I wouldn't do too much of that, Annie.

ANNIE: Wouldn't you? I would.

TOM: Sorry. I didn't mean to shock you. Did I shock you, telling you that?

ANNIE: Yes.

TOM: Oh. Sorry. Anyway, that's why he's drunk. He's been let down by . . .

ANNIE: By his bit on the side? Well, lucky him.

[TOM *wanders to the window.* ANNIE *glares at* REG *who whistles nonchalantly.* ANNIE *wanders to sit, passing* REG *and kicking him in the shin as she does so.* REG *clasps his leg and continues to whistle though in some pain.*]

TOM: He's still up there. The cat. Think he's staging some sort of protest.

ANNIE: Oh, forget the damn cat.

TOM: Think I'll switch on the outside lights, if you don't mind. Might encourage him down, when it gets dark.

[TOM *goes out to the garden for a second.*]

REG: Sarah making the coffee, is she?

ANNIE: She was fighting for the privilege. Literally.

TOM: [*returning*] Lovely evening. Going to be quite a sunset. Really quite something . . . You know, I don't think I altogether got the point of that vet joke.

REG: Never mind, never mind.

ANNIE: You haven't been telling him jokes again?

REG: I tried my best.

ANNIE: You never learn, do you? And no more rows between you and Sarah, please.

REG: I didn't do anything. Just standing there, she flung this tin of biscuits at me . . . oh, don't talk about biscuits, I'm starving.

ANNIE: She probably had good cause.

REG: Nonsense.

ANNIE: Must remember to give Mother her medicine in fifteen minutes.

TOM: It's on a night like this, you know, one could really fancy going out and sleeping under the stars. Used to do that when I was at College.

REG: Didn't it have a roof then?

TOM: Yes. I meant, in the vacations. I used to take my tent and bicycle off somewhere.

REG: Yes, great that. Get a group of you together . . .

TOM: No, no, mostly on my own. Preferred it. I did take someone one year but we didn't really hit it off. He was very—ebullient—I think that's the word. I don't honestly think you can possibly share a small tent for any length of time with someone who's ebullient. I remember he used to lie there in his sleeping-bag, night after night, whistling under his breath. Maddening. It was no good saying anything to him because he had a frightful temper. He couldn't bear it if you criticized him. He'd take it very personally. Practically go berserk. I remember, he once threw my canvas bath on the camp fire. Just because I said something he didn't care for. So I mostly went on my own. Watched for badgers. Impossible to watch badgers with a man like that. Anyway, he failed his finals . . .

[NORMAN *snores*.]

ANNIE: Oh, no, we're not going to have to put up with that all evening, are we?

TOM: Yes. A whole canvas washstand. On the fire. Ruined it.

REG: If she hadn't flung those biscuits at me, we could have had those.

[NORMAN *snores*.]

ANNIE: Norman, shut up.

[SARAH *comes in with the tray of coffee etc.*]

SARAH: Here we are. Sorry I took so long. I had to rinse the cups again. Someone who shall be nameless had put them away without . . .

[NORMAN *snores*.]

Oh, my God, what's that?

ANNIE: Guess who.

SARAH: Oh no, this is too much. I'm not having this. Norman, get up this minute. Norman—

REG: Save your breath, he can't hear you. He's bubbling over with dandelion wine.

SARAH: Revolting. Well, we can't leave him there, for heaven's sake.

REG: He's all right.

SARAH: He is not all right.

REG: He isn't in anybody's way. Leave him alone.

SARAH: I am not sitting down to have coffee with that all over the floor.

REG: [*irritated*] Well, what are we supposed to do with him?

ANNIE: [*swiftly*] All right. All right. We'll move him. That's enough. We'll move him. Tom . . .

TOM: Um?

ANNIE: Give me a hand.

REG: No. I'll do it. It's all right.

[REG *and* TOM *heave* NORMAN *half up by his arms.*]

[*To* SARAH] Now then, Madam, would you like him wrapped or will you take him as he is?

ANNIE: [*indicating easy chair*] Put him here.

SARAH: [*watching them deposit* NORMAN] Absolutely revolting behaviour.

REG: There you go . . .

ANNIE: [*at coffee*] What's everybody want? White or black?

SARAH: No, I'll do it . . .

ANNIE: It's all right.

SARAH: No. I'm doing this—

ANNIE: I'm already doing it.

SARAH: You're not already doing it, I'm doing it.

ANNIE: Oh, don't be so ridiculous, Sarah.

SARAH: I'm not being ridiculous. This is your weekend to rest.

ANNIE: Oh, forget that.

SARAH: Will you please give me that coffee pot?

ANNIE: What's the use of—

SARAH: Annie, will you give me that coffee pot at once or I shall lose my temper?

ANNIE: [*thrusting the pot at* SARAH] Oh, go on have the damn thing then. [*She sits sulkily.*]

SARAH: Thank you. [*Recovering her composure*] Now then, everyone. Black or white?

REG: I should heat it up first. It'll be cold by now.

SARAH: [*ignoring him*] Tom?

TOM: Um?

SARAH: Coffee?

TOM: Oh, thanks very much.

SARAH: Thank you, Tom. Black or white?

TOM: Um . . . [*A pause.*]

SARAH: Annie?

ANNIE: No, thank you.

SARAH: Oh don't be so silly.

ANNIE: None for me, I couldn't drink it.

SARAH: Reg?

TOM: Black, I think.

SARAH: I'm asking Reg.

TOM: Oh. Sorry.

REG: White.

SARAH: Please.

REG: Please.

SARAH: At last. White for Reg. Black for Tom. None for Annie.

TOM: I think I'll change mine to white on second thoughts.

[SARAH *gives him a glare*. NORMAN *snores*.]

SARAH: Is there any way of stopping that noise? [*Holding out two cups to* TOM] Would you mind, Tom?

[TOM *hands one cup to* ANNIE *who gives it to* REG.]

SARAH: Well now, how would we all like to spend this evening?

[*A silence*.]

It's not often we're all gathered together like this. I'm sure we can . . .

[NORMAN *snores*.]

. . . think of something.

[*A silence*.]

REG: Well, I thought it might be quite fun if we were to have a go at my game, perhaps.

SARAH: I'm sure nobody wants to do that.

REG: It'd be quite fun.

SARAH: We don't want to waste our evening doing that.

REG: You may not but—

SARAH: No one does, don't be so boring.

REG: [*muttering*] I just thought if . . .

SARAH: We hardly see each other at all. One of the few occasions we all manage to be together, away from that blessed television and without the children to worry about —wouldn't it be rather nice if for once we could just sit and have a pleasant civilized conversation?

REG: Civilized conversation?

SARAH: Yes, why not?

REG: We couldn't have a civilized conversation if we tried. Hark at you just now. You were only pouring the coffee out, there was practically a bloody civil war.

SARAH: Well, I'm not wasting my time playing your silly games and that's final. [*Silence*.]

ANNIE: I think I'd quite enjoy a game.

REG: Ah!

SARAH: What?

ANNIE: And I'm sure Tom would. Wouldn't you, Tom?

TOM: Um?

ANNIE: You'd like to play Reg's game, wouldn't you?

TOM: [*doubtfully*] Oh—

SARAH: Of course he doesn't, do you Tom?

ANNIE: Of course he does, don't you Tom?

TOM: Er— [*Looking from woman to woman*] Well . . .

ANNIE: Super. Come on then, Reg.

REG: [*already unpacking the board*] If you're sure you'd like to . . .

ANNIE: Tom . . .

TOM: Yes, all right.

REG: You going to play, Sarah?

SARAH: Well, I suppose if it's a choice between that and sitting on my own . . .

REG: Grand. We'd better pull the table out. Give us a hand, Tom.

[TOM *and* REG *pull the table to the centre of the room.* ANNIE *puts four chairs round it.* SARAH *stands and watches.*]

SARAH: I'm not playing for long. I think I'll have an early night.

REG: It's all right, it's quite a quick game.

SARAH: I've heard that before.

TOM: [*helping* ANNIE *with the chairs*] That one of yours we played before was very complicated.

REG: [*starting to lay out the game*] Ah, you mean my mountaineering one.

TOM: Yes. I seem to remember I kept running out of sherpas.

REG: Ah well, you didn't buy enough sherpa cards to start with. You need the sherpas to carry your oxygen.

TOM: Yes, I ran out of that as well. My whole expedition was a total write-off.

SARAH: Well, let's play this game, shall we, if we're going to?

REG: Yes, right. Well, sit where you like. Sarah, you go there and Annie . . .

SARAH: I can't sit here. The board's upside down. I can't read it.

TOM: Sit here.

ANNIE: No, she can sit here.

REG: No, it's all right, I'll turn the board round, it's very simple.

SARAH: Now you can't read it.

REG: I don't need to read it, I know.

TOM: I think I can read it sideways all right.

[SARAH *now sits opposite* REG. ANNIE *opposite* TOM.]

ANNIE: It looks very exciting. [*Picking up a pile of cards*] What are these?

REG: [*anxious*] No. Don't touch anything.

ANNIE: Sorry.

REG: I'll explain.

SARAH: Well, I hope it doesn't take all night.

REG: Right now.

SARAH: Don't forget Mother's medicine, will you Annie?

ANNIE: Five minutes yet.

REG: Right now. This is the board.

TOM: Go slowly, won't you? I'm not awfully quick on these sort of things.

SARAH: Hah!

ANNIE: You don't say.

TOM: [*a bit nettled for him*] I do my best, I do my best.

REG: Well just listen. Listen carefully. This board represents the street map of a city. Each of these areas marked brown are buildings.

TOM: Buildings.

REG: Now, as you see, they are all marked very clearly what they are. These are shops, you see. Greengrocers . . . outfitters . . . bank and then along here jewellers . . . dress shop.

TOM: What's this here? Coop. What's a coop?

REG: Co-op.

TOM: Oh, Co-op. I see. Sorry . . . reading sideways, you see.

ANNIE: Oh Tom, for goodness sake.

TOM: All right . . . don't keep on at me, don't keep on at me, there's a good girl.

ANNIE: Well, honestly, you're so slow!

REG: And all these grey areas are the roads.

SARAH: Oh, this is far too complicated to learn in one evening.

REG: It's not complicated if you'll listen. Now the object of the game is as follows.

SARAH: I mean, it takes an hour just to read the—

REG: [yelling] Listen!

NORMAN: [waking up with a jerk, loudly] Wah! Wah! [Everyone reacts.]

SARAH: Oh my God.

NORMAN: I was having a terrible dream. It was a terrible dream, you've no idea.

ANNIE: You all right, Norman?

NORMAN: Hallo. There was this great big black shape and it was coming after me—like a cloud—only it was making this buzzing noise. [He demonstrates with a buzzing noise.]

REG: [over this] We're having a game at the moment, Norman.

NORMAN: And I was trying to run away from it. But you know how it is in a dream, your feet won't move—

TOM: I've had that.

REG: Yes, terrible. Now, the object of the game . . .

NORMAN: [threshing his feet about] You're running, running but you're still in the same place. You know you're dreaming but you can't wake up. Terrifying. You came into it, Sarah . . .

SARAH: Yes, I think you'd better lie down.

ANNIE: You can use my bed, if you like. I'll make up the spare one later.

SARAH: No, Norman can sleep on the spare one.

ANNIE: No, it isn't made up.

SARAH: Then I'll make it up.

REG: Oh, come on we're playing a game.

TOM: Is this blue thing a road?

REG: No, that's a river.

TOM: Ah.

SARAH: Are the sheets in the linen cupboard?

ANNIE: Sarah, if you don't mind, I'll deal with it.

SARAH: There is no need for you to, you're supposed to be having a rest—

[NORMAN *has risen and blundered into her in the doorway.*] Where are you going?

NORMAN: Phone. I've got to phone.

ANNIE: [*indicating phone*] Well, use this one.

NORMAN: Oh yes.

SARAH: Who are you phoning?

NORMAN: My wife. Ruth. I need to speak to my wife. I demand to speak to my wife . . .

REG: Well, phone in another room, there's a good chap . . . [*Knocking* TOM'*s hand from the board*] And don't fiddle with those . . .

TOM: Sorry.

ANNIE: He'll have to phone in here. The other one's in Mother's room—God, it's nearly time for her medicine—

NORMAN: I want to speak to Ruth.

ANNIE: [*soothingly, guiding him to the phone*] All right, Norman—here. Sit here. You can phone from here.

NORMAN: Thank you very much.

ANNIE: Can you manage?

NORMAN: God bless you and keep you.

SARAH: Do you think it's wise, him speaking to Ruth?

ANNIE: No idea.

SARAH: Probably upset her more than ever.

ANNIE: [*returning to the table*] Probably.

REG: Sarah, are you playing or not?

SARAH: [*sitting*] Yes, all right, all right. Let's get it over and done with.

REG: We haven't even started. Now then, the object of the

game is as follows. With four players, two of us represent the police, and two of us, the criminals . . .

NORMAN: [*on the phone*] Hallo . . .

REG: Now, the aim of the criminals . . .

NORMAN: Ruth? It's me . . .

REG: . . . is to plan a successful raid . . .

NORMAN: Me. Norman. I'm at Mother's.

REG: [*with a glare at* NORMAN] . . . on any shop they choose. The aim of the police . . .

NORMAN: Your Mother's. Of course, your Mother's . . .

REG: The aim of the police, obviously, is to stop them.

NORMAN: How the hell can I be at my Mother's? She's been dead for ten years . . .

REG: Norman . . .

NORMAN: Well, don't say it in that tone.

REG: Norman . . .

NORMAN: God, can't we even have a—excuse me a minute. [*Covering the mouthpiece, to* REG] What's that?

REG: Could you keep it down a bit?

NORMAN: Beg your pardon. [*Into phone, softly*] Yes?

REG: Thank you. The aim of the police is to stop the raid and capture the crooks red-handed . . .

NORMAN: [*softly into phone*] Yes, yes. I know . . .

REG: Is that clear so far?

SARAH: Perfectly clear, do get on with it.

TOM: Um . . .

REG: I don't think Tom's got it. You followed it so far, Tom?

TOM: I think so. Police and crooks, yes. The bit that still worries me is this river. It seems to be running straight through the Co-op. Is that right?

REG: It runs underneath it. Underneath.

TOM: Oh, I see. Better not shop in the basement.

REG: [*vastly irritated*] Oh, for heaven's sake . . .

ANNIE: Oh, Tom, do shut up.

TOM: [*irritably*] All right. All right . . .

NORMAN: [*loudly into phone*] I said, you're a selfish bitch.

[*As the others turn, covering mouthpiece*] Sorry . . . sorry. [*Into phone, softly*] What? Yes . . . yes.

SARAH: Come on, Reg, get on with it.

REG: I am trying to get on with it. Now. The police can spot the criminals as follows. They have three police cars— [*holding up a model car*] which are these. Police cars can run on the roads but not in the buildings . . .

SARAH: That's a relief.

REG: Look, do you mind, do you mind? The police cars can see up to twenty spaces ahead of them and up to four spaces each side. They can't see behind them and they can't see round corners.

SARAH: Why can't they see behind them?

REG: Because they can't, that's why.

TOM: Motto: don't drive behind a police car.

NORMAN: [*loudly for a second*] Love? What do you know about love . . .? [*with an apologetic look at the others, continuing in a lower tone*] Have you ever felt love for a single human being in your life?

REG: The police also have the Chief Superintendent. [*Holding him up*] This chap . . . He can see up to three spaces ahead of him and three spaces round a corner . . .

TOM: Useful chap in a crisis.

SARAH: Oh, this is absurd.

REG: What's absurd?

SARAH: How can you have a man see three spaces ahead and three round a corner?

REG: Because he's got a very long neck. I don't know, it's a game, woman.

SARAH: It's not even realistic.

REG: What's that got to do with it?

SARAH: It's not much of a game if it's not even realistic.

REG: What are you talking about? Realistic? [*Leaping up*] What about chess? That's not realistic, is it? What's wrong with chess?

SARAH: Oh well, chess . . .

REG: In chess, you've got horses jumping sideways. That's

not realistic, is it? Have you ever seen a horse jumping sideways?

SARAH: Yes, all right . . .

REG: [*leaping about*] Like this. Jumping like this. That's very realistic, I must say.

SARAH: You've made your point.

ANNIE: Reg . . .

REG: And bishops walking diagonally. [*Demonstrating again*] You ever seen a bishop walking like this? Well, have you? I'm asking you, have you ever seen a flaming bishop walking like this?

SARAH: Reg, will you please sit down and get on with it.

REG: [*sitting, triumphantly*] Well then.

NORMAN: Don't you hang up on me—Ruth! Ruth! [*He jangles the receiver up and down*] Hallo? Hallo? What? Who's this? Mother . . . what are you doing on the line, get off.

SARAH: Who's he talking to?

NORMAN: Ruth! Hallo . . . Mother, will you please get off this line?

ANNIE: Oh, my God. He jiggled the receiver . . .

NORMAN: Mother!

ANNIE: He rang the extension bell in Mother's bedroom.

NORMAN: [*into the phone*] Look—would you shut up, both of you, for a minute and let me get a word in . . . Mother, if you don't hang up, I'll come and sort you out personally.

ANNIE: [*moving to* NORMAN] Norman . . .

NORMAN: [*into phone*] What did you say? [*To* ANNIE] Go away.

ANNIE: Norman—please . . .

NORMAN: All right, Mother, I've warned you . . . I'll come up and wrap it round your neck . . .

[NORMAN *bangs the receiver down on the table and strides out.*]

SARAH: Norman . . .

ANNIE: Norman!

SARAH: Stop him . . .

ANNIE: Norman!

[ANNIE *goes out after* NORMAN.]

SARAH: [*following her*] Well, don't just sit there . . .

[SARAH *goes out after* ANNIE.]

REG: I wonder if the bloke who invented Monopoly had this trouble . . .

TOM: Very difficult to concentrate. [*He rises, wanders to the phone, picks up the receiver and listens*] Good grief . . .

REG: What's happening?

TOM: There's a heck of a rumpus on the extension . . . yelling their heads off . . . hallo? Who's that? Ruth? Oh, hallo, Ruth it's Tom . . . yes, Tom . . . fine . . . how are you? . . . oh . . . oh . . . oh, I see . . . oh, I'm sorry, yes . . . oh dear . . . oh dear . . . [*He pulls a face at* REG] Oh yes . . . how dreadful . . . yes . . .

[ANNIE *returns breathless.*]

ANNIE: Tom, Reg, for goodness sake. Leaving us to cope with Norman. He's practically attacked Mother. He's out of control.

REG: Well, I don't see that . . .

ANNIE: Tom!

TOM: What? . . . just hang on a second, Ruth . . . [*To* ANNIE] What?

ANNIE: Tom, would you stop standing there looking so useless and do something for once in your life . . .

TOM: What?

ANNIE: I've never met anyone so useless . . .

TOM: Now look here, I wish you'd stop going on at me like this. You're damned lucky to have me around, you know.

ANNIE: Oh really?

TOM: Yes, really. Every time anything goes wrong, you seem to take it out on me. First of all, it's your holiday, then it's Norman . . . well, it's just not on, it really isn't.

ANNIE: Um?

REG: Won't somebody play with me, please . . .

TOM: The next time you're planning holidays for two, if you want me along, perhaps you'd be good enough to be polite enough to ask me.

ANNIE: You've got a hell of a nerve.

TOM: And anyway, if you want to be seen with me, you'd better smarten yourself up a bit. You're a mess, you know. You look like something that's fallen off a Post van.

ANNIE: I beg your pardon?

[NORMAN *returns*.]

NORMAN: [*crossing straight to phone*] That's settled that.

ANNIE: Norman . . .

NORMAN: [*into phone*] Ruth? Hallo? . . . she's hung up. Would you believe it, she's hung up on me.

TOM: I'm going home, I'm fed up. Just count yourself lucky I don't belt you one and give you rabies.

[TOM *strides out*. SARAH *enters with her blue bedjacket now in two halves*.]

SARAH: Look what you've done. Look what you've done to my bedjacket.

NORMAN: [*collapsing*] Nobody loves me. Nobody loves me any more.

ANNIE: Norman . . .

SARAH: Look at this. Will somebody look at this?

REG: Won't anybody play with me? Please . . .

Curtain

ACT TWO

Scene One

The sitting room. Sunday 9 p.m. RUTH *stands by the window.* REG *sits at the table fiddling with his game.*

RUTH: I shouldn't have wasted my time coming down here. Norman makes these gestures regularly. And every time I fall for them. We've been married for five years, I really ought to know better. As a result of his hysterical phone call last night, I have not been able to do a stroke of work at home today and will probably lose my job tomorrow, when I finally turn up. I almost wish to heavens he'd gone away with Annie, had his weekend and got it over with. Instead of involving everyone else. Mind you, that would be much too simple for Norman. No point in making a gesture unless he has an appreciative crowd to applaud him. [*Looking at her watch*] Too late to drive back now. I think I'll go to bed in a minute.

REG: I'm amazed you two are still together.

RUTH: Well. I think other people's marriages are invariably a source of amazement. They usually are to me. I mean, you and Sarah . . . You know, I have found quite often it's the people you look at and say, well they won't last long, who cling on grimly till death. Maybe they're so aware of public opinion, they're determined to prove it wrong. You and Sarah—me and Norman—and Annie and that —Tom man. Though I think Norman's successfully knocked that on the head.

REG: Tom's gone home, then?

RUTH: I saw him stamping off into the night. Probably the most constructive thing Norman's done for some time. Saved Annie from a fate worse than marriage. A sort of eternal engagement.

REG: I don't know. He's nice enough, Tom.

RUTH: Not nice enough for her. Oh—this house! I feel like

getting a paint brush and going over it with red and orange and bright blue. It's like a brown museum. A very dirty brown museum.

REG: Well, you can't expect Annie to—

RUTH: No, I don't expect Annie to do anything. She's got enough to cope with, with that—evil woman upstairs.

REG: Never got on with Mother either, did you?

RUTH: No. She never liked me, I never liked her. Mutual.

REG: We were saying earlier, you and Mother were rather alike.

RUTH: [laughs] Maybe . . .

REG: I wouldn't say Sarah and I were altogether incompatible. We have differences. I won't try and hide that. We certainly have differences. But you know, six of one . . . She's pretty good with the children. On her good days. Runs the house very well. Better than you or Annie would. Or Mother.

RUTH: Of course, she does have the advantage of you running round in circles for her.

REG: That's all right, I don't mind. I prefer being told what to do really. I often think if nobody told me what to do I'd never do anything at all. I remember she went away once for a fortnight. When her father was ill. Took the children with her. Left me on my own in the house. Do you know I felt myself gradually slowing down. At the end of ten days I was hardly moving at all. Extraordinary. It was as if she'd wound me up before she left and now I was running down. I hadn't even got the energy to take the milk in. Sarah reckons I've got some rare tropical disease. Burmese inertia, or something. Anyway, it's better to be calm with Sarah. She's like those toy animals you see in the back windows of cars. Any violent movement from me and she's nodding her head reproachfully for days. It works out all right. Most days.

[ANNIE *comes in. She sits.* RUTH *now studies one of* SARAH's *magazines.*]

RUTH: Who's washing up?

ANNIE: Nobody. I'm not, so nobody is. I've done quite enough this weekend. I'm not doing any more.

RUTH: Good for you.

REG: I'll do it in a minute.

ANNIE: No, don't. You did it last night. Somebody else can do it.

RUTH: You looking at me?

ANNIE: Or Norman. Or Sarah.

RUTH: Ha!

REG: Huh!

ANNIE: I don't know who ever does anything in your house. You and Norman are both as bad as each other.

[RUTH *continues to read her magazine, holding it a few inches from her nose.*]

What are you doing?

RUTH: Trying to read.

ANNIE: You can't read like that. It's resting on your nose.

RUTH: I like the smell of newsprint.

ANNIE: Why don't you wear your glasses?

RUTH: I can manage thank you.

ANNIE: If you don't like glasses, you could get contact lenses.

RUTH: I tried them. They don't work.

ANNIE: Of course they do.

RUTH: They weren't designed for people who share a house with Norman. Life with him is full of sudden, unexpected eye movements. They kept falling out . . . where the hell did you get all these dreadful magazines?

REG: They're Sarah's.

RUTH: Oh. I do beg her pardon.

[*A pause.*]

REG: Tom's gone home.

ANNIE: Yes.

REG: Ah.

[*A pause.*]

He'll be back tomorrow, I expect.

ANNIE: I doubt it. Even he has a limit.

REG: Oh, he'll be back.

RUTH: It's not altogether our fault if he doesn't come back.

ANNIE: What, after the way everyone's treated him? All right, I know I haven't been particularly nice either—but that was different. I don't know why I'm so mean to him sometimes. It's just when you're fond of someone—you worry what other people think of them. You want them to be something they're not capable of being. Which is very unfair on them really. I mean, he's Tom isn't he? That's one of the best things about him. He's always Tom. He never pretends. He never puts on an act for anybody.

RUTH: No, he's always Tom. You're right there.

ANNIE: Well it's better than living with an emotional big-dipper like Norman.

RUTH: Depends on your tastes, doesn't it?

ANNIE: I know which I'd prefer.

RUTH: Then I should stick to it then if I were you.

ANNIE: All right. I'm sorry. We have been through that. Norman caught me when I was very depressed. The tail end of that awful Christmas. He asked me at a time when I hardly knew what I was doing.

RUTH: There's no need to explain. He's always been an expert at timing—whatever else. He proposed to me in a crowded lift. It was total blackmail. He sounded so appealing he won the sympathy of everyone round us. Had I been heartless enough to refuse him, they'd have probably dropped me down the lift shaft. I managed to stall him for three floors and then the lift man said, sorry folks, nobody gets out till the little lady says yes. I remember that was the first time I really felt like throttling Norman.

REG: Very romantic. I proposed to Sarah just out there in the garden, you know.

ANNIE: Yes, we know. Ruth and I watched you through the window.

REG: You didn't, did you?

RUTH: We weren't going to tell him.

ANNIE: Oh, what's it matter now ... Sarah was all wobbly and quivering, trying to make up her mind and Ruth kept saying say no, say no.

REG: Thank you.

ANNIE: I must see to Mother in a minute.

RUTH: If it's not too tackless a question, how long is she going to remain like that?

ANNIE: Oh, for ever. Well, till she dies.

RUTH: Is that what Dr Whatsisname says?

ANNIE: Wickham says there's no reason why she shouldn't last for years. Most of it's psychosomatic. Well, we knew that anyway. She just has no desire to get up. No reason to. So she doesn't. Sad really. Her whole life was centred round men, wasn't it? When they lost interest in her, she lost interest in herself. I hope I never get like that.

RUTH: No danger. Don't worry.

ANNIE: Oh well, yes, I know I'm not quite the femme fatale figure but ...

RUTH: I mean that, thank God, you can see a bit further than she ever could. That woman never had a thought in her head in her life. Look at her, lying up there reading those dreadful books.

ANNIE: I'm afraid if I'm here alone with her much longer, I might start to get like her. You know, when I went up to her this afternoon, I had this dress on and a bit of make-up—she was so gleeful. She thought at last her propaganda was beginning to have an effect.

RUTH: Well, we'll try and come down more often. If we can. But I've got Norman and Reg has got Mrs Reg and all the little Reggies. You do see.

ANNIE: If you could try.

RUTH: Yes, we'll try. Won't we, Reg?

REG: What? Oh yes. Bit of a job getting away but I'll see what Sarah can arrange.

[SARAH comes in.]

SARAH: Well. [She sits.] Nice and quiet for once.

ANNIE: Yes ...

SARAH: What are you doing, Reg?

REG: I'm just . . .

SARAH: Oh. Haven't you got anything to do?

REG: I'm doing something.

SARAH: Yes . . . well, don't be too anti-social will you?
   [*A pause.*]
   I've got Norman doing the washing up.

RUTH: You've what?

ANNIE: You've really been working the charm.

SARAH: No, I just had to ask him. I said would he be very
   kind since I wasn't feeling really up to it and . . . he was
   perfectly agreeable.

RUTH: You must pass on the secret. Everything that can fall
   to bits in our house has done so. All the doorknobs come
   off in your hand. None of the cupboards open, three of
   the windows are stuck, the fridge needs a plug and on wet
   days, we have to climb out of the front room window to
   go to work because the front door warps when it rains. I
   could probably do it myself but I'm damned if I'm going
   to.

SARAH: If you don't mind my saying so, I think you just
   handle Norman wrongly. If you ask him nicely, he's very
   willing and helpful.

ANNIE: That's good coming from you. You always say he's
   impossible.

SARAH: I think we underestimate Norman.

ANNIE: What have you been up to out there?

SARAH: What do you mean?

RUTH: Better change the subject.

SARAH: I don't know what you mean.
   [NORMAN *enters with the salad basket.*]

NORMAN: Excuse me.

REG: Hey hey. The domestic man.

NORMAN: Liberated to the kitchen.

ANNIE: Just sling it on top of the cupboard.

NORMAN: Sling it, right.

ANNIE: Just gently, Norman, don't get carried away.

NORMAN: Right ho, Chief.

[NORMAN *salutes and goes.*]

RUTH: What a revolting sight. What have you done with the slob I married?

ANNIE: She's house trained him at last.

RUTH: That I doubt. [*Rising*] Well, on that awful picture I'm off to bed. Which room was Norman untidying last night?

ANNIE: The spare room. Reg's old one.

RUTH: Right. Tell Norman, if he wants to join me he may. But I'd prefer it if he came on his own. [*Waving magazine at* SARAH] May I borrow this to read?

SARAH: Of course.

RUTH: It's so gruesome, it should frighten me to sleep. Goodnight all.

ANNIE: Do you want a call in the morning?

RUTH: If you sleep with Norman, you wake at dawn. Be warned.

[RUTH *goes out.*]

SARAH: Goodnight.

REG: Night.

ANNIE: Night.

SARAH: Personally, I think if she showed Norman a little more kindness and encouragement she might find him a little less difficult . . .

ANNIE: Well, don't let one success go to your head.

SARAH: Let's face it, Ruth's always had difficulty getting on with anybody. Most of the time she doesn't try.

[*Unseen by* SARAH, RUTH *returns for her handbag.*]

I'm sure Norman's difficult to live with. I've no doubt. But any man who had to live with Ruth for any length of time . . .

[REG *clears his throat.*]

No, I mean honestly I . . . [*She tails off as she sees* RUTH.]

RUTH: Goodnight.

[RUTH *goes out.*]

SARAH: [*in an undertone*] She did that deliberately.

REG: [*rising*] Well, I think I'll follow on. Do you mind if I go in the bathroom first?

SARAH: No.

REG: Got to drive in the morning. Get an early night.

SARAH: Would you switch on the blanket, dear?

REG: Right. Do you want a bottle?

SARAH: No, it's too mild for a bottle. I just want the chill off the sheets. They seemed a little damp last night.

REG: Right. [*He pecks* SARAH *on the cheek*] See you up there then.

SARAH: All right.

ANNIE: Night, Reg.

SARAH: I don't know when we'll get down here again. I think we're very booked up between now and Christmas.

ANNIE: Oh well, if you can. You know . . .

SARAH: It would be so much easier if we could bring the children . . .

ANNIE: Well do, there's room for them.

SARAH: Oh, no. They'd disturb Mother.

ANNIE: She wouldn't mind. She'd like to see them.

SARAH: No. I don't think so, really. They're very noisy. We'll all come down again at Christmas, if Mother's any better. [*Pause.*] I hope Tom isn't too upset.

ANNIE: Don't know.

SARAH: I expect he'll be back.

ANNIE: Expect so.

SARAH: I mean, he must realize it wasn't anything serious between you and Norman.

ANNIE: Maybe, maybe.

SARAH: I mean, as Norman says, it was just an idiotic idea of his.

ANNIE: Did he say that?

SARAH: Yes, he was saying in the kitchen, it was nothing in the least serious. He just thought you looked a bit tired and fed up and needed a change. Act of charity, really.

ANNIE: Oh. Is that what he said?

SARAH: Nothing for Tom to get jealous about.

ANNIE: No.

SARAH: Why don't you go up to bed too. You're looking very washed out.

ANNIE: I have to see to Mother first.

SARAH: I'll tell you what, I'll see to Mother. You get an early night for once.

ANNIE: All right. You may have to read to her, I warn you.

SARAH: I don't mind. I'll read to her.

ANNIE: You wait till you see what she reads.

SARAH: [*hustling her along*] All right then, come on, up you go.

ANNIE: Yes, I'm going.

SARAH: What's Mother due for, now?

ANNIE: [*consulting her watch*] Er—nine thirty. Two green ones and one pink if she'll swallow it. Try and persuade her to. She's got a thing about the pink ones for some reason. She says they make her giddy.

SARAH: [*hurrying to the door*] Two green, one pink. [*Turning*] Coming?

ANNIE: Yes. All right. I'm coming . . .

SARAH: [*hovers for a second, then reluctantly gives up*] Well. Don't stay down too long. Goodnight.

ANNIE: Night.

[*She stands indeterminately. She wanders to the window and looks out unhappily.*]

Oh. Hell . . .

[*She goes to the bookcase.*]

Read it—read it—read it—read it . . .

[*She goes to the pile of magazines and starts to select one.*
NORMAN *comes in with a saucepan.*]

NORMAN: Er—oh.

ANNIE: On the wall. Over the draining board, there's a hook.

NORMAN: A hook. Right. Everyone gone to bed?

ANNIE: Yes.

NORMAN: It's too bad, you know, I'm slaving away out here . . . Ruth gone to bed?

ANNIE: Yes. She said you're welcome to join her.

NORMAN: Oh.

ANNIE: Which I think is very reasonable of her really. I'm not sure I'd be as generous.

NORMAN: You've really gone off me, haven't you?

ANNIE: Just a bit, Norman, yes.

NORMAN: What can I do?

ANNIE: I think we don't talk about it. I think we just keep out of each other's way. You'll be going home tomorrow morning then we can forget all about it.

NORMAN: I was going to take you away, you know.

ANNIE: I don't want to talk about it, Norman.

NORMAN: I would have done. I was ready. I had it all planned. It was you. You said—

ANNIE: [at the door] Goodnight, Norman.

NORMAN: Annie. Just a second, please . . .

ANNIE: [turning] Goodnight.

NORMAN: I didn't mean to mess it up for you and Tom, I really didn't.

ANNIE: That's all right. You didn't.

NORMAN: But he's gone off.

ANNIE: I did that myself.

NORMAN: Then why are you blaming me for it?

ANNIE: Because as I say, Norman, I feel like I've been taking part in one of Reg's games. Only in this case, you and Ruth are making up all the rules as you go along.

NORMAN: What's Ruth got to do with it? She would never have known.

ANNIE: Until you phoned her.

NORMAN: I only phoned her when you changed your mind. I got drunk. I was unhappy. Oh, Annie, I wanted this weekend for you. I wanted it to be . . .

ANNIE: An act of charity.

NORMAN: What?

ANNIE: Nor do I like you discussing me in the kitchen with Sarah. Making out you'd taken pity on me, for God's sake.

NORMAN: Who told you that?

ANNIE: Sarah told me. If you want a secret kept don't tell Sarah in future.

NORMAN: I only said that to calm her down. You know what Sarah's like. Gets all het up . . .

ANNIE: I'm going to have an early night, Norman, I'm off.

NORMAN: I was really looking forward to our weekend, you know.

ANNIE: So was I.

NORMAN: Sorry.

ANNIE: Not all your fault.

NORMAN: Another time, eh?

ANNIE: Not on your life.

NORMAN: Oh. If I booked early enough, I could perhaps get us into Hastings next year.

ANNIE: Oh Norman.

NORMAN: I mean, not that there's anything wrong with East Grinstead but . . .

ANNIE: Goodnight.

NORMAN: Annie.

ANNIE: What?

NORMAN: Can I kiss you goodnight?

ANNIE: No.

NORMAN: Can I kiss you goodbye then? Please.

ANNIE: Norman. You are definitely evil.

NORMAN: I love you.

ANNIE: No.

NORMAN: Kiss?

ANNIE: Not until you take that back.

NORMAN: What?

ANNIE: That you love me. It's not true. Don't say it.

NORMAN: All right. I don't love you. Can I have a kiss, please?

ANNIE: Okay. Come on.

[NORMAN *hesitates*.]

Come and get it if you want it.

NORMAN: Don't say it like that.

ANNIE: Well, how am I supposed to say it?

NORMAN: Well. Nicely. Like you did at Christmas.

ANNIE: All right. Kiss me, Norman.

NORMAN: No.

ANNIE: What?

NORMAN: Come over here, first. On our rug.

ANNIE: Now don't you start that.

NORMAN: No, no. Just a kiss. Promise.

ANNIE: I don't trust you.

NORMAN: Look, I'm holding a saucepan.

ANNIE: What's that got to do with it?

NORMAN: I've only got one hand.

ANNIE: I seem to remember you can do a lot with one hand.

NORMAN: Promise.

ANNIE: Just one kiss.

NORMAN: Yes.

ANNIE: [*moving to him*] Goodnight and goodbye, Norman. [*They kiss. A little longer than* ANNIE *had planned.* NORMAN's *saucepan flails in the air.* SARAH *enters. She carries a pill bottle. She sees* ANNIE *and* NORMAN. *She pauses for a second and then, banging down the bottle, advances furiously and swiftly across the room.* NORMAN *sees her over* ANNIE's *shoulder and tries to pull out of the kiss, with a muffled warning. He is too late.* SARAH *grabs* ANNIE *by the shoulder and shoves her away from* NORMAN.]

SARAH: You deceitful little whore. Get upstairs. Get up to bed this instant.

ANNIE: [*amazed*] Who do you think you're talking to?

SARAH: [*shoving* ANNIE *again*] Get upstairs! Go on . . .

ANNIE: And, please, I do not like being pushed around.

SARAH: I will push you around just as much as I—

ANNIE: You will not, you know.

SARAH: [*pushing* ANNIE *again*] Get upstairs, do you hear me? Get upstairs.

ANNIE: I warn you, Sarah, you push me once more, I'll slap your stupid face.

NORMAN: I say—

ANNIE: And you can shut up too, Norman.

SARAH: You're a really nasty piece of work, aren't you? All that innocent little girl act. You're just a tart like your Mother.

ANNIE: Sarah, I will not have you talking about my Mother like that.

SARAH: Dirty little slut.

ANNIE: If you call me any more names . . .

SARAH: Slut, slut.

ANNIE: [*raising a rather impressive looking fist*] You asked for it. [ANNIE *advances menacingly on* SARAH. SARAH *retreats grabbing an ornament by way of a shield.*]

SARAH: Don't you come near me. Don't you dare threaten me.

ANNIE: Then take it back. [RUTH *enters. She is now dressed only in an old dressing gown,* NORMAN'S. *She stands for a moment bemused, taking in the scene:* ANNIE *and* SARAH *about to come to blows and* NORMAN *beginning to enjoy every minute of it.*]

SARAH: I will not take it back. You're a tart and a slut.

ANNIE: Don't you call me that, you frustrated bitch.

SARAH: Keep away. Keep away . . .

ANNIE: I'll wring your stupid neck.

RUTH: [*thundering*] Annie! Sarah! That's enough. [*A silence.*] All right, that's enough.

SARAH: [*quite hysterical*] She has no right to say that to me.

RUTH: [*sharply*] I said that's enough. Goodnight, Sarah.

SARAH: If you'd seen what she . . .

RUTH: Goodnight, Sarah. [SARAH *goes to the door, gives a last indignant glare back into the room and goes out.*] Goodnight, Annie.

ANNIE: [*going slowly to the door*] Goodnight.

NORMAN: [*lamely*] Night. [ANNIE *goes out. A very long silence.* RUTH *seems lost for words. She opens her mouth to speak to* NORMAN, *then doesn't. She walks*

*up and down. She sits. She opens her mouth to speak to him again.
She can't. She gets up and walks about some more.*]

RUTH: [*finally*] Do you ever realize, Norman, the number of
times in a day I could lose my temper with you and don't?
[NORMAN *continues to study his toes and saucepan.*]
I usually manage by some supreme effort of will to control it. Well this time, I'm sorry, I'm quite unable to.
[*Moving to him*] You understand what I'm saying, Norman? I am simply bloody livid. [*She slaps his face.*]

NORMAN: Ow.

RUTH: How could you, Norman, how could you do it?
Don't you think it was bad enough for me at Christmas
to lie there ill in bed? Knowing you were down here playing around with one woman. But two.

NORMAN: [*muttering*] I wasn't playing with two.

RUTH: Why do you do it? Don't you have any feeling for me?

NORMAN: I don't know, I'm just—

RUTH: Just what?

NORMAN: I'm just magnetic or something.

RUTH: You are not magnetic, Norman. Not at all. You are
odious. You are deceitful, odious, conceited, self-centred,
selfish, inconsiderate and shallow.

NORMAN: I'm not shallow.

RUTH: Have you anything to say at all? Anything?

NORMAN: That's my dressing gown, isn't it?
[RUTH *moves around agitatedly for a second.*]

RUTH: I don't know what to say. I just don't know what to
say . . . And stop looking like that, for heaven's sake.

NORMAN: Like what?

RUTH: Giving me that awful doggie look of yours. It may
work wonders with those two but it does nothing for me.
I've seen it far too much.
[RUTH *sits away from him.* NORMAN *wanders unhappily.*]
Well, I think this is it, don't you? I think this is where we
say thank you very much, goodbye. On top of everything
else you've made me look a complete fool . . . [*Peering
round*] Where have you gone, I can't see you?

NORMAN: Over here.

RUTH: Oh. No, I think you're just comtemptible.

NORMAN: [*edging towards her and finally touching her hand*] I'm sorry.

RUTH: Don't.

NORMAN: I am.

RUTH: Let go of my hand.

NORMAN: I am.

RUTH: Will you let go of my hand?

NORMAN: Why?

RUTH: Because I don't want you touching me.

NORMAN: Oh. [*He wanders away*] So you want me to go, do you?

RUTH: I think it's the only thing left.

NORMAN: For you.

RUTH: And for you. You're obviously not made to be married. You never were. Stupid of me to try and make you behave like a husband in the first place. You'd be much happier if you were perfectly free, flitting from woman to woman as the mood takes you.

NORMAN: I don't do that.

RUTH: You'd like to.

NORMAN: I know the real reason.

RUTH: Reason for what?

NORMAN: Why you want to get rid of me. Because I interfere with your work. That's why you'd like to get rid of me.

RUTH: Talk about turning the conversation. You really are the limit.

NORMAN: Well . . .

RUTH: That isn't true either.

NORMAN: Which comes first then? Which comes first? Work or me?

RUTH: You do. Did.

NORMAN: Work or me?

RUTH: I've said, you.

NORMAN: Work or me?

RUTH: I'm not going on with this.

NORMAN: You can't can you? You know it's not true.

RUTH: We'll talk about this in the morning. You can sleep down here.

NORMAN: Where?

RUTH: I don't know. In a chair. You're certainly not coming up with me. I refuse to be number three in a night.

NORMAN: Nothing happened you know. They both just started fighting. I was just saying goodnight to Annie and then Sarah attacked her.

RUTH: Oh yes, really? How interesting. That sounds so terribly likely.

NORMAN: It's true. You're the only one, Ruth. You know that.

RUTH: I certainly don't.

NORMAN: Well, you should know that. You should know me by now. I mean, this whole weekend was—for you.

RUTH: For me? What do you mean it was for me?

NORMAN: It was a gesture for you.

RUTH: Really.

NORMAN: Of course it was. You know that.

RUTH: [*studying him*] I don't think you're any of these things I said you were. You're just stupid.

NORMAN: Possibly.

RUTH: You just don't think. You want locking up.

[RUTH *goes to the door. She stops. She turns.*]

All right then.

NORMAN: What?

RUTH: Come on. Come upstairs if you're coming. I must be half-witted but still . . . [*She waits*] Come on.

NORMAN: [*smiling*] Here a minute.

RUTH: What?

NORMAN: Just come here a second.

RUTH: [*moving in slightly*] What for?

NORMAN: Please . . .

RUTH: [*moving in further*] Why?

NORMAN: [*beckoning her in*] Bit closer . . . closer . . . that's it.

RUTH: Now, I'm not in the mood for games Norman.

NORMAN: No. That's it . . . [*He draws her to him and kisses her*] I love you.

RUTH: You really are the most . . .

[NORMAN *starts to pull her down onto the rug.*] What are you doing?

NORMAN: I suddenly had this wonderful idea.

RUTH: What?

NORMAN: On the rug. Come on, on the rug.

RUTH: What?

NORMAN: On the rug. Come on.

RUTH: Norman, no . . .

NORMAN: It's nice on the rug . . . come on, on the rug.

RUTH: Norman . . . really . . .

NORMAN: There. Isn't it nice on the rug?

RUTH: Norman . . .

NORMAN: Oh, Ruth . . .

RUTH: It's nice on the rug.

NORMAN: I told you it was. It can be our rug.

RUTH: Norman . . .

[*The lights fade as they enjoy the rug and each other.*]

Curtain

ACT TWO

SCENE TWO

The sitting room. 8 a.m. Monday morning. RUTH *and* NORMAN *now rolled up in the rug asleep.* NORMAN's *jacket is a pillow.* REG *enters without seeing them. He carries two suitcases. He places one on the floor, puts the other on the table and starts packing away his game.* RUTH *opens her eyes and yawns loudly.* REG *jumps. He turns and sees her.*

REG: Flipping heck!
RUTH: Reg . . .? [*Realizing where she is*] Oh, my God. Norman. Norman, wake up you fool . . .
NORMAN: [*instantly awake*] What—what—what—morning —what?
RUTH: Norman . . .
NORMAN: Oh—oh, God. Hallo Reg. Ruth, we've over-slept. [*He starts to try to get up.*]
RUTH: [*yelling*] Don't unroll the rug yet. Wait a minute.
NORMAN: Sorry. Oh yes . . .
[RUTH *and* NORMAN *wriggle about under the rug adjusting their dress.*]
RUTH: [*as they do so*] You don't really have to stand there gaping, do you, Reg?
REG: Oh, no. Sorry, no. Morning.
RUTH: [*satisfied that her dressing gown is again covering her*] All right.
NORMAN: Right. [*They unroll from the rug.*]
RUTH: Honestly. [*She gets up*] You fool, Norman. Why didn't you wake up? Please, Reg, don't say anything to anyone will you? I beg you. I'll never live it down.
REG: No—no—
RUTH: Honestly, Norman, you fool. Why didn't you wake up?
[RUTH *goes out.* NORMAN *smiles amiably at* REG.]
REG: I take it you two have patched up your little

differences?

NORMAN: My wife and I have come to an agreement.

REG: Good.

NORMAN: [*getting up*] Lovely morning—oooh! She's been lying on my arm. Oooh, oooh, oooh. [*He shakes his arm which flaps uselessly.*] Wouldn't tell anybody about this.

REG: No.

NORMAN: Otherwise they'll all want to do it.

REG: Don't think I fancy it. Prefer my bed. Despite the wife. [*He laughs.*]

NORMAN: [*putting on his jacket*] You're off then?

REG: She seems to be hurrying me along for some reason, yes. What was the matter with her last night, do you know?

NORMAN: Who?

REG: Sarah. She came to bed shaking. I've never seen her so bad. I mean, literally shaking. The whole bed was vibrating for hours. Like sleeping on top of a spin dryer.

NORMAN: It must have been the overexcitement.

REG: What overexcitement?

NORMAN: No idea.

REG: Not much of that this weekend was there? Well, the old arguments but that's usual. I must say, on the whole, I've enjoyed the rest.

NORMAN: Yes. Good to get out to the countryside occasionally.

REG: You're right there.

[SARAH *comes in with a bag.*]

SARAH: Reg, have you brought those—? Ah, yes—oh. [*She sees* NORMAN.]

NORMAN: Morning.

SARAH: [*cool*] Good morning. [*To* REG] What are you doing?

REG: Just packing. Just packing.

SARAH: Oh, we're not lugging that all the way home with us again, are we?

REG: I'm not leaving it here. This took me months to make.

SARAH: We're never going to have time for it, Reg.

REG: It's all right, I think I've adapted it now so I can play on my own.

SARAH: And you promised to take these magazines up to Mother.

REG: I will. I'm going to. I'll have my breakfast first.

SARAH: And we can't waste too much time over that, either. [*Coldly to* NORMAN *who's blocking the way out*] Excuse me please. [SARAH *goes out.*]

REG: What's the hurry? We're in a hurry. I don't think she's forgiven you yet, by the look of it.

NORMAN: No.

REG: No. Very cool. Got a long memory has Sarah. It'll be a few months before you're back in favour.

NORMAN: Ah well. I'll try and win her round.

REG: No chance. You'll be told when you're forgiven and not before. She doesn't talk to me for days on end sometimes. Amazing how she remembers to keep it up. I mean, if I have a row in the morning, when I come home in the evening I've forgotten all about it. Until I open the front door. Then it hits you straightaway. Atmosphere like a rolling pin. Know what I mean? She's got great emotional stamina, my wife.

NORMAN: So have I.

REG: You'll need it. Good luck.

[NORMAN *goes out.* REG, *alone, whistles a tune. He closes his suitcase. He puts it on the floor next to the other, wanders to the centre of the room, looks at the rug and laughs. He wanders to the window and stares out.*]

Oh, hallo. What are you doing out there?

[TOM *comes in rather tentatively.*]

TOM: Ah . . .

REG: What were you doing hiding out there? Thought you were a cat burglar. [*He laughs.*]

TOM: No. Er—thought I'd just look in, you know. I was on my way to—somewhere—and I thought I'd look in.

REG: Come in.

TOM: Thank you.

REG: Nice day again.

TOM: Um?

REG: Lovely.

TOM: I'm afraid I flew off the handle last night.

REG: Oh, don't worry.

TOM: I shouldn't think I'll be very welcome here today.

REG: Whyever not? Don't worry . . .

TOM: I didn't sleep at all. Turning it over in my mind, you know. I mean, let's face it. What claim have I got to Annie? None at all. Why should I kick up a fuss—if somebody else . . .

REG: It's natural. Human nature.

TOM: I shouldn't have blown my top.

REG: I don't honestly think a lot of people noticed.

TOM: Really?

REG: No.

TOM: I was very boorish.

REG: Well . . .

[ANNIE *comes in dressed as in Scene One.*]

ANNIE: Oh. Hallo.

TOM: Hallo.

ANNIE: There's some tea and stuff in there, if you want it, Reg.

REG: Oh, right ho. Wonderful.

ANNIE: Not a lot but—

REG: Right. [*Pause.*] I think I'll take these up to Mother. Before I forget. Otherwise Sarah'll be on to me again. Excuse me.

[REG *picks up the pile of magazines and goes out.*]

TOM: Yes. I must be getting along I think. I was just—

ANNIE: Tom.

TOM: Yes.

ANNIE: Stay a minute.

TOM: All right. [*He looks at his watch.*] Yes, fine. [*He looks at his watch again.*] Fine. I came to apologize really.

ANNIE: What for?

TOM: Well for—yesterday—losing my temper and—general things.

ANNIE: No need to apologize.

TOM: No, I know there isn't. Everyone keeps telling me that. But I think an apology's due. I came to give it. To you.

ANNIE: Thank you.

TOM: Well. [*He looks at his watch.*] Well . . .

ANNIE: Do you want a cup of tea before you go?

TOM: Oh. If there's one going. Won't say no. Didn't feel like breakfast when I got up. Felt a bit sick actually but—er . . .

ANNIE: Come on then.

TOM: You think they'll—er . . . welcome me in there?

ANNIE: Whyever not? Come on.

[*she starts to lead* TOM *out. They pass* RUTH *coming in, now dressed.*]

TOM: Oh, Ruth I—er . . .

RUTH: Oh hallo, Tom, good morning. You're bright and early.

TOM: Ruth, I . . .

RUTH: Mmm?

TOM: I—er . . . nothing.

RUTH: What's wrong?

ANNIE: Nothing's wrong. Come on.

TOM: Right.

[NORMAN *enters as they go out.*]

NORMAN: Hallo. Good morning Mr Vet. [*He slaps* TOM *on the back.*]

[TOM *and* ANNIE *go out.*]

You're dressed.

RUTH: I wasn't going home in your dressing gown. I've come up in a rash. I think it was from that rug.

NORMAN: Really? That's unusual.

RUTH: What do you mean unusual? Do you make a habit of rolling people on the rug?

NORMAN: No.

RUTH: No?

NORMAN: No. You look fabulous this morning.

RUTH: I look simply dreadful. I couldn't see my face. I haven't had a bath. I feel terrible.

NORMAN: I love that dress. It's great.

RUTH: It's the same one I had on yesterday.

NORMAN: Is it?

RUTH: I only brought one with me. I didn't plan to spend the night in the hearth. I suppose you want me to drive you home now?

NORMAN: Yes please.

RUTH: I have to go to work.

NORMAN: You'll have to go home first, you can't go to work like that. You look a dreadful mess.

RUTH: Yes. You're supposed to be at work too.

NORMAN: I was taken ill, haven't you heard?

RUTH: I'm amazed they keep you on.

NORMAN: I'm a very good librarian, that's why. I know where all the dirty bits are in all the books.

RUTH: We'd better say goodbye.

NORMAN: No breakfast?

RUTH: You can get something at home. If there is anything —which I doubt.

NORMAN: What would you say—if I asked you a favour?

RUTH: What sort of favour?

NORMAN: Would you take the day off and stay at home?

RUTH: No.

NORMAN: Not even with me?

RUTH: Especially not with you.

NORMAN: Please.

RUTH: Norman, I am doing a full time job. I just can't—

NORMAN: I could ring up for you. I could say you were ill.

RUTH: No.

NORMAN: Oh, why can't you be ill for once? Go on, be ill. I know. I'll pretend I'm the doctor. I'll say, I'm phoning up on behalf of Mrs Dewers. I have just examined this woman on the rug. She has an ugly rash and in my opinion, she's in great need of some attention. Attention from

who, you may ask. [*He springs at her.*] Attention from
me.

RUTH: Norman . . .

NORMAN: Kiss.

RUTH: Norman. [*She kisses him.*]

NORMAN: Are you happy?

RUTH: What?

NORMAN: Do I make you happy at all?

RUTH: Well . . .

NORMAN: Say you're happy.

RUTH: Why? Is it important?

NORMAN: Yes. I want you to be happy. I want everyone to
be happy. I want to make everyone happy. It's my mis-
sion in life . . .

RUTH: Yes all right, Norman. Well, let's not worry about
other people too much, just concentrate on making me
happy, will you? The other people will have to try to be
happy without you, won't they?

NORMAN: But you are happy?

RUTH: Yes. I'm fairly happy.

NORMAN: And you might possibly—feel ill—if you drove
very fast all the way home and—somebody made you a
cup of tea and—made the bed and—ran you a bath and
—put in the bath salts and—

RUTH: Yes. I might.

NORMAN: How are you feeling?

RUTH: Dreadful.

NORMAN: [*with a great cry of joy*] Ha-ha! [*He grabs her and
whirls her around.*]

[REG *enters.*]

REG: Oh, blimey, they're at it again.

[RUTH *breaks from* NORMAN *as* SARAH *and* ANNIE *come
in.*]

SARAH: Well, I think we're ready to go.

REG: One piece of toast. One piece of toast. How can I drive
on one piece of toast?

ANNIE: Have you got everything?

SARAH: I think so. Did you take our sponge bag out of the bathroom, Reg?

REG: Yes, yes, yes.

RUTH: Well, I'm going to see if I can start the car.

NORMAN: Right. [*He starts to put on his mac and hat.*]

RUTH: Oh Norman, you don't have to put all that on.

NORMAN: I prefer to travel incognito.

RUTH: You've still got that suit on. It isn't even yours.

NORMAN: Oh yes. Can I borrow this, please?

ANNIE: Well, Father doesn't need it any more. You might as well.

RUTH: It doesn't even fit him.

NORMAN: I could do with a new executive suit.

RUTH: Come on. [*To* SARAH, REG *and* ANNIE *in turn*] Goodbye. Goodbye. Goodbye.

ANNIE: Bye, Ruth.

REG: Bye, bye.

SARAH: Goodbye.

RUTH: [*going*] I'm in the car. I'm leaving in ten seconds.

NORMAN: All right. All right. [*To* ANNIE] Goodbye. Thank you and . . .

ANNIE: [*fairly cool*] Goodbye, Norman.

NORMAN: Reg.

REG: So long.

NORMAN: Sarah.

SARAH: [*warmly*] Goodbye, Norman. Have a good journey. See you at Christmas, I hope.

NORMAN: Like the mistletoe, I shall be here.

RUTH: [*off*] Norman!

NORMAN: Bag. Where's my bag?

REG: This it?

[NORMAN *goes for it.*]

RUTH: [*off*] Norman!

SARAH: [*going to the door and calling*] He's just coming, Ruth, he's just coming.

REG: She's forgiven you very quickly, hasn't she?

NORMAN: You think so?

REG: What did you say to her?

NORMAN: Nothing. I just cheered her up a bit. Bye bye. Goodbye Annie. Goodbye Sarah.

RUTH: [*off*] Norman, I have left.

NORMAN: All right, all right, I'm coming.

[NORMAN *goes*.]

REG: Well. Nice to see him but I'm glad it's only twice a year.

SARAH: Yes, I think it's time we were . . . Goodbye, Annie. [*She pecks her cheek*.] Take care, won't you?

ANNIE: And you. Have a good journey.

REG: Thank you.

ANNIE: You won't mind if I don't come and see you off, will you? I must get back to Tom. He's sitting there waiting. He's decided he'd like breakfast after all.

SARAH: Oh yes, you go back to Tom.

REG: I told him not to worry about this weekend. I did right, did I? To tell him that?

ANNIE: Yes.

REG: Hope everything works out.

ANNIE: Expect so.

SARAH: [*at window*] Norman's having to push that car of theirs.

REG: Want a tip? Take Tom out there. Sit him under the tree. Good place to make a proposal out there.

ANNIE: It worked for you.

REG: Yes.

ANNIE: I'll try it. One of these days. Bye bye.

SARAH: Goodbye Annie dear.

REG: Bye love.

[ANNIE *goes out*.]

SARAH: Oh, I am fond of this garden. Even though it's overgrown. Oh, just look at Norman. What does he think he's doing? [*She laughs*.]

REG: Could do with a lot of work. I thought they were still paying someone to look after it. That old man. He's worse than useless. No one keeps an eye on him. So he doesn't do a stroke.

SARAH: As long as the sun's shining, I'm happy.

REG: Are you?

[SARAH: *stands smiling serenely*.]

You're very cheerful.

SARAH: Why shouldn't I be?

REG: No. No reason. Carry on.

SARAH: Can you manage those?

REG: [*gathering up cases*] Just about.

[*Pause*.]

SARAH: I wonder what Bournemouth would be like at this time of year?

REG: Bournemouth?

SARAH: Yes . . .

REG: What made you suddenly think of Bournemouth?

SARAH: It just occurred to me.

REG: You don't want to go to Bournemouth, do you?

SARAH: Not now . . .

REG: I thought we were going home.

SARAH: Not now. Sometime. I think I'd rather fancy it. Next year—perhaps.

REG: All right. I'll take you. If it'll make you happy.

SARAH: No, you don't need to bother. I could go on my own easily.

REG: On your own?

SARAH: Leave you in peace for a bit. Just for the weekend. Be rather nice to get away. For a weekend . . .

REG: Don't know why you want to go to Bournemouth. Why Bournemouth? Why not make it Brighton? Or Worthing? [SARAH *goes out*.] Or Reigate, for that matter? Or East Grinst—

[*He pauses. An awful thought*] Oh, my God. Sarah! Wait for me, love. Sarah . . .

[REG *hurries out with his cases*.]

Curtain

ROUND AND ROUND THE GARDEN

Characters

REG
SARAH, his wife
RUTH, Reg's sister
NORMAN, her husband
ANNIE, Reg and Ruth's younger sister
TOM

Scene: The Garden

Time: A weekend in July

ACT ONE

SCENE ONE

The garden. Saturday, 5.30 p.m. Overlooked by a Victorian, country vicarage-type house with terrace and doors leading directly into the sitting room. Once obviously well laid out, it is now wildly overgrown. The other way off leads down through the wilderness to the lane at the bottom and can also take you round to the front of the house.

TOM, a pensive, thoughtful man, enters. Casually dressed in weekend country clothes. He stands gazing rather aimlessly about him. After a moment, ANNIE enters. Red faced and shiny, she wears a very old sweater, button-up and too large, jeans and gum boots. She stops as she sees TOM.

ANNIE: [*casually*] Oh, Tom. Hallo.

TOM: Hallo, Annie.

ANNIE: Didn't know you were here this afternoon.

TOM: Yes. I thought I'd just look up your cat if I could. See that paw of his.

ANNIE: Oh, yes, fine.

TOM: I put a dressing on it but it's probably come off by now.

ANNIE: Probably.

[*A pause.*]

TOM: Lovely day.

ANNIE: Yes.

TOM: You'll be going off soon, I take it.

ANNIE: Yes.

TOM: Oh. Have a good time.

ANNIE: Thanks.

TOM: Don't get lost.

ANNIE: I can't get far in a day. Any sign of Reg and Sarah?

TOM: Haven't seen them.

ANNIE: Hope they're not going to be late. I'll have to hang on till they come just to make sure they know where everything is for Mother.

TOM: Yes.

ANNIE: She's been lying up there moaning all day because I'm going away. You'd think I was off for a year, instead of a couple of nights.

TOM: I'll look in if you like. Make sure they're coping.

ANNIE: They'll manage.

TOM: Nice of them to offer, wasn't it?

ANNIE: Sarah and Reg?

TOM: Yes.

ANNIE: Why shouldn't they? She's his mother too, after all. It's high time they did offer. They get off very lightly. So does Ruth for that matter. They're all perfectly happy to leave me to cope for nine-tenths of the year. The least they can do is to spare me a couple of days. Not that I'll ever get Ruth to do anything. Far too busy with her high finance. But Reg and Sarah are perfectly capable . . .

TOM: Quite.

ANNIE: What will you be doing?

TOM: When?

ANNIE: This weekend.

TOM: Oh, you know. Mooching about.

ANNIE: On your own?

TOM: Probably.

ANNIE: That's what I'll be doing.

TOM: Ah. Well, I'll think of you, wherever you are, mooching about while I'm—mooching about here.

ANNIE: Thanks. [Pause] Silly really.

TOM: What?

ANNIE: Well—both of us in different parts of the country, stuck on our own . . .

TOM: Yes. Funny thing, life.

ANNIE: Yes. [Pause] What's the time?

TOM: Er—just gone five-thirty.

ANNIE: Oh.

TOM: When are you leaving?

ANNIE: I'm catching the bus in the village. That's providing Reg and Sarah arrive in time.

TOM: I can run you down in the car.

ANNIE: No—

TOM: If you look like being . . .

ANNIE: No, I'd rather walk.

TOM: Won't you have a case?

ANNIE: No. It's all right. I don't mind carrying suitcases. I quite enjoy it. The walk . . .

TOM: Oh. Any idea where that cat is?

ANNIE: Probably outside here somewhere. I must get on. Prepare for my lone trip.

TOM: See you before you go then.

ANNIE: Yes.

TOM: Better search out my patient. [*Calling*] Pussy, puss, puss . . .

[TOM *goes off.* ANNIE *stands for a moment looking after* TOM.]

ANNIE: [*at length, exasperated*] Oh . . .

[ANNIE *goes off the other way. A pause. Birds sing.* NORMAN *enters stealthily. Despite the bright sunshine of the late July afternoon, he has on a rather grimy mac and a woolly hat. He is bearded, a rather aimless sort of beard. He carries a battered cardboard suitcase. Not surprisingly, he is perspiring furiously. As the house comes into his view, he stops, smiles to himself, puts down his case and, at peace with the world, breathes in the country air.*]

TOM: [*off, distant*] Kitty—kitty—kitty . . . cat—cat—cat . . . kitty—kitty—kitty . . .

[NORMAN, *on hearing this, dives swiftly for cover, forgetting his case, which he leaves standing in the middle of the path.* TOM's *voice fades into the distance.* NORMAN *remains hidden.* ANNIE *enters. She clumps along the terrace, carrying roses she has evidently just picked. She stops as she sees* NORMAN's *case. She approaches, curious, and stares at it. She looks about her.*]

ANNIE: Hallo? Anyone about?

NORMAN: [*hidden, muffled*] Annie . . . [ANNIE *stares about her.*] Annie . . .

ANNIE: Norman?

NORMAN: [*bounding from his cover, ecstatic*] Annie!

ANNIE: Oh . . . you've come . . .

NORMAN: Yes.

ANNIE: But what are you . . .?

NORMAN: I couldn't wait. I had to see you.

ANNIE: But we agreed . . . Oh, Norman, honestly. You are the limit . . .

NORMAN: [*passionately*] Oh, my darling . . . [*He moves romantically to her but stops suddenly. With a cry*] Oh—God!

ANNIE: [*alarmed*] What's the matter?

NORMAN: These bloody brambles . . . Why doesn't somebody clear these bloody brambles?

ANNIE: Hang on—stop flailing about . . . [*She takes his hand to pull him clear.*]

NORMAN: [*yelling*] Don't pull! Don't pull! It's impaled in my leg.

ANNIE: [*bending to free him*] All right. Wait—wait . . .

NORMAN: Aaaah!

ANNIE: Ssh.

NORMAN: You must have hands like asbestos. [*As ANNIE frees him*] Aaah! Aaah! Aaah! [*Hopping away and sitting*] God!

ANNIE: Mother's resting you know. You'll wake her up.

NORMAN: [*rolling up his trouser leg*] Look at this. I'm scratched right down my leg.

ANNIE: If Mother's woken up before she's ready to wake up, she doesn't know where she is. It takes me an hour to explain . . .

NORMAN: Look, blood—bleeding . . .

ANNIE: Let's see. [*She bends to look.*]

NORMAN: Careful! Deformed for life.

ANNIE: Hold these— [*She hands NORMAN the roses.*]

NORMAN: [*taking them and dropping them immediately with another yell*] Aaah!

ANNIE: Ssh.

NORMAN: It's a death trap, this garden.

ANNIE: Look, will you please be quiet.

NORMAN: Only been here two minutes, lost three pints of blood. [*He sucks his hand.*]

ANNIE: Oh, Norman do shut up. You're so weedy.

NORMAN: [*indignant*] Weedy?

ANNIE: A real weed. [*She starts to pick up the flowers.*]

NORMAN: [*romantic again*] Oh, Annie . . . [*He reaches out and touches her leg.*]

ANNIE: [*pulling away, irritated*] Don't. Just a minute.
[NORMAN *stares at her a second, then lies back.*]

NORMAN: I'm exhausted.

ANNIE: I should think so. In that coat.

NORMAN: It was raining in Fulham.

ANNIE: Was it?

NORMAN: Metaphorically it was.

ANNIE: Oh.

NORMAN: [*expansive*] Ah, the sun, the sun, the sun . . .

ANNIE: Norman . . .

NORMAN: Mmm?

ANNIE: What are you doing here?
[NORMAN *laughs secretively.*]
No, seriously Norman. What's the point of our making all these arrangements, of trying to make absolutely sure no-one was going to get upset—no-one was going to get hurt—and then you turn up here.

NORMAN: I wanted to see you. I was frightened you'd changed your mind.

ANNIE: But I'm supposed to meet you. We're supposed to meet. In the village, at the back of the Post Office, seven o'clock.

NORMAN: I got here early.

ANNIE: Well, you'll have to go away for an hour . . . I haven't even packed.

NORMAN: Where am I supposed to go?

ANNIE: I don't know. Go and walk round the Abbey.

NORMAN: That's five miles away. I'm not walking five miles, just to wander round some ruin with a suitcase.

ANNIE: I don't want you here when Reg and Sarah arrive. And I've got to see them in. I've got to show them where everything is for Mother. All her bottles and pills and God knows what. And which is their towel. I mean, there's masses. I can't just rush off. Anyway, Tom's here . . .

NORMAN: [*scornful*] Tom.

ANNIE: He's only round the front of the house, looking for the cat.

NORMAN: Tom. Ha!

ANNIE: And don't say it like that. I don't say Ruth, ha!

NORMAN: I don't mind if you do. I say it.

ANNIE: Not to her face, you don't.

NORMAN: How do you know?

ANNIE: I bet you don't. I've seen you with her.

NORMAN: How do you know what I say to her face behind your back?

ANNIE: I know you. More important, I know my sister.

NORMAN: She'll have got my note by now.

ANNIE: Note?

NORMAN: Telling all.

ANNIE: All what?

NORMAN: It's all over between us. That ever since we stayed here last Christmas, something wonderful happened. You and I were all that mattered. That everything else . . .

ANNIE: You didn't? You didn't say that?

NORMAN: That the love between us—

ANNIE: If you said that, I warn you, I'll ring her up this minute . . . [*She moves away.*]

NORMAN: [*alarmed*] Where are you going?

ANNIE: To ring her up.

NORMAN: All right, all right. I didn't. I didn't leave her a note. Promise.

ANNIE: Promise?

NORMAN: Promise.

ANNIE: So long as you haven't. I mean—well, after all she is my sister. I'm fond of her. Quite. We've already agreed it's stupid to—upset everything just for us. We're being terribly adult, aren't we? You said we were—in your letter . . . Far better we two just go away quietly to a little hotel somewhere, get it all off our chests—out of our system—God, I'm making it sound like a laxative—you know what I mean—work it all off, that's what I mean. Then you go back to Ruth and live happily ever after— or as happily as you can seeing it's Ruth and I come back to Mother and—and—look after her . . .

NORMAN: And then? When your Mother finally pegs out?

ANNIE: Oh well. I'll face that when it comes.

NORMAN: Yes, you'll have to.

ANNIE: There's Tom. He's hovering in the background.

NORMAN: The creeping vet.

ANNIE: He's done a lot to help here, you know. He did all the kitchen ceiling for me. Two coats . . . He's a jolly good vet too. He has a marvellous way with animals. Actually, he's better with them than he is with people really.

NORMAN: You'll have to start going around on all fours then, won't you?

ANNIE: Oh, shut up. I don't know why you're so nasty about him, he likes you very much.

NORMAN: He takes you for granted. Here you are—a beautiful girl. Vibrant. He could marry you tomorrow. He could make you happy. And what does he do? He spends more time with that cat than he does with you.

ANNIE: Well, he's a vet isn't he?

NORMAN: Vet. V.E.T. Very Egocentric Twit. He doesn't deserve you.

ANNIE: And you do?

NORMAN: No. But I'm strangely engaging.

ANNIE: No, you're not, you're foul. I don't think I want to come with you after all. I've changed my mind. I'll give Mother a blanket bath, it'll be much more fun.

NORMAN: I love you.

ANNIE: Oh, Norman . . . When you look like that, I almost believe you. You look like a—what are those things . . .?

NORMAN: Greek gods.

ANNIE: Old English sheepdogs.

NORMAN: Oh, great.

ANNIE: They're super dogs. All woolly and double-ended.

NORMAN: I'm not woolly and double-ended.

ANNIE: You are a bit. You're like a badly built haystack.

NORMAN: I'm going.

ANNIE: Yes, you'd better before Tom . . .

NORMAN: [*taking her hand, suddenly very serious and intense*] Goodbye, my darling.

ANNIE: [*suppressing her laughter*] Oh, Norman, do stop it.

NORMAN: What?

ANNIE: Oh, I'm sorry, I— [*She starts laughing.*]

NORMAN: [*hurt*] What?

ANNIE: It's just you're so—terribly quaint.

NORMAN: [*huffily*] If it's quaint to be romantic . . . I mean, if you prefer me to knock you down . . .

ANNIE: Try it.

NORMAN: If that's what you want. Where's the romance? Where's the romance gone? Destroyed by the cynics and liberationists. Woe betide the man who dares to pay a woman a compliment today . . . he bends to kiss her hand and wham—the old karate chop on the back of the neck and she's away with his wallet. Forget the flowers, the chocolates, the soft word—rather woo her with a self-defence manual in one hand and a family planning leaflet in the other.

ANNIE: Oh, Norman, you are stupid.

NORMAN: Yes. I really do love you, Annie.

ANNIE: Do you?

NORMAN: Yes.

ANNIE: That's a pity.

NORMAN: Why?

ANNIE: For everyone. Golly, look at this garden. It's like a jungle. Old Mr Purdy's got his leg again. He's been off a fortnight.

NORMAN: [*disinterested*] Oh.

ANNIE: Mrs Purdy says it's a war wound, but I think it's gout. He's a terrific drinker. All day. The potting shed's full of his empties. He says they're for weed killer but he's got enough there to defoliate the whole of Sussex. If you look out of the window at tea time, you can see him draped over his spade. Like an old bag of fertiliser . . .

NORMAN: Seven o'clock then, back of the Post Office. [*He goes to move.*]

ANNIE: Seven o'clock. I say, it's awfully exciting in a way, isn't it? I mean, do you know I haven't been away from this place for nearly two years, what with Mother and one thing and another. I'm longing to see the sea again. I've forgotten what it looks like.

NORMAN: Ah.

ANNIE: Where did you say we were going? Hastings. Why did you choose Hastings?

NORMAN: Well . . . it looks sort of close on the map.

ANNIE: I'm not complaining. I mean, I'm sure Hastings is super.

NORMAN: Yes. As a matter of fact, I wasn't able to get a vacancy after all—not in Hastings.

ANNIE: Oh.

NORMAN: It's summer, you see.

ANNIE: Yes, I've noticed.

NORMAN: Ah, well, I'd forgotten.

ANNIE: So we're not going to Hastings?

NORMAN: I'm afraid not.

ANNIE: Where are we going?

NORMAN: Well, I managed after a bit of trouble to get us fixed up in East Grinstead. They had a cancellation.

ANNIE: [*digesting this*] Oh, well. Super. East Grinstead, then. I haven't been there, either.

NORMAN: It was the best I could do. It's on the way to Hastings.

ANNIE: Lovely.

NORMAN: [*leering*] Not that we'll see much of it—eh?

ANNIE: [*blank*] How do you mean?

NORMAN: Well . . .

ANNIE: Oh. [*Doubtful*] Oh yes. [*She thinks*] I expect we'll want some fresh air at some stage though, won't we? I mean, we won't—all the time. I mean, if it's a hotel they'll want to make the beds and—change the soap—so I expect we'll get time for a bit of a snoop around, just a bit.

NORMAN: [*unconvinced*] Oh, yes . . .

ANNIE: It'd be a shame to go all the way to East Grinstead and then not see anything of it at all. I mean, what the hell, let's do what we said and have a really *dirty* weekend. I mean, absolutely *filthy* but, you know, if it's all . . . makes Jill a dull girl. [*She laughs*] God, I'm putting this awfully badly.

NORMAN: You've just pulled a button off.

ANNIE: Mmm?

NORMAN: Your woolly thing. You've just pulled the button off.

ANNIE: [*finding it in her hand, absently*] Oh yes. [*She puts the button in her pocket.*]

[*They are both embarrassed now.*]

NORMAN: I stopped off in the village. Bought some new pyjamas.

ANNIE: Oh. Super. In my honour?

NORMAN: Yes.

ANNIE: Better than wearing the same ones you do with Ruth.

NORMAN: Yes.

ANNIE: I mean, just because you're unfaithful there's no need for your pyjamas to be as well.

NORMAN: No.

ANNIE: I'm afraid you'll have to put up with my sensible flannelette. They're quite pretty but they're going round the knees and elbows.

NORMAN: Ah.

[*A pause.*]

ANNIE: Well.

NORMAN: Yes.

[*A pause.*]

Would you like to have a look at my pyjamas now?

ANNIE: Well, I—

NORMAN: A sort of sneak preview.

ANNIE: I think I'd rather wait until— [*She pauses. Listens*] Was that the bell?

NORMAN: Bell?

ANNIE: Ssh. Mother's bell. She's awake. Now, you must go. See you at seven. [*As she hurries into the house*] I'll have a bath before I leave.

[ANNIE *goes in.* NORMAN *stares after her. He stands looking uncertain. He opens his case and removes a pair of cellophane-wrapped pyjamas. He stares at them critically. He places them on a bush and steps back to see what effect they have from a distance.* TOM *comes back. He is staring up into the trees.*]

TOM: Kitty—kitty—kitty. Cat—cat—cat . . . [*He spies the cat up a tall tree*] Ah, there you are . . .

[NORMAN *is staring in disbelief.*]

Oh, hallo Norman. Didn't know you were here.

NORMAN: Tom.

TOM: You and Ruth down to lend a hand, are you?

NORMAN: How do you mean?

TOM: With Annie going away. Are you down to help out?

NORMAN: More or less.

TOM: Where's Ruth?

NORMAN: She's not here.

TOM: Oh. I thought you said she was.

NORMAN: No, I never said she was. You're the one who said she was.

TOM: [*deciding he's lost the thread of this conversation*] Look at that daft animal.

NORMAN: Mmm?

TOM: See it? The cat—up there.

NORMAN: Oh yes.

TOM: [*calling*] Avoiding me—aren't you? [*To* NORMAN] Septic paw.

NORMAN: Uggh.

TOM: Last time I looked at it, we two had a mild disagreement. [*To cat*] Didn't we? Yes. [*To* NORMAN] Not the most sociable animal.

NORMAN: Vicious brute. Kills on sight for pleasure.

TOM: Well, I can't really treat a patient who's thirty foot up a tree. Think I'll call it a day. No way of luring him down.

NORMAN: You could sling a brick at it.

TOM: Hardly.

NORMAN: Breach of professional etiquette?

TOM: Something of the sort. [*Seeing* NORMAN's *pyjamas*] Good Lord, what on earth are those?

NORMAN: Sssh. They look like wild pyjamas. Don't disturb them, they're nesting.

TOM: Yours, are they?

NORMAN: Yes. I'd better put them away before they savage someone. [*Snatching them and cramming them back in his suitcase*] Go on, get in you brutes. In, in—get in. [*He slams the lid triumphantly*] The tops are all right, it's the bottoms you've got to watch.

TOM: [*impressive through this*] Seen Annie yet?

NORMAN: No. Yes. Why?

TOM: Well. What's your opinion?

NORMAN: What of?

TOM: Man to man? Between you and me?

NORMAN: What?

TOM: I mean, it's very odd, isn't it?

NORMAN: What is?

TOM: Her holiday. I mean, there's nothing wrong in having a holiday, but why the mystery?

NORMAN: Mystery?

TOM: Practically sneaking off. Won't say where she's going. What she's going to do.

NORMAN: Perhaps she doesn't want people to know.

TOM: Not like Annie, that. She's usually very open. Frank sort of person. No secrets. Know what I mean?

NORMAN: Really?

TOM: I mean, I've known her a long time—

NORMAN: That doesn't give you ownership of her.

TOM: No. Gives me interest. Concern.

NORMAN: I should stick to coaxing cats out of trees.

TOM: [*thoughtfully*] Hastings.

NORMAN: Eh?

TOM: I've got a feeling she's set her sights on Hastings.

NORMAN: Oh?

TOM: She keeps bringing it up. In passing. You know—"Do you think it'll be warm in Hastings at this time of year?" —that sort of thing. Sometimes she tries to confuse the scent. Makes it Deal or Brighton. But Hastings is the commonest. I'm betting even money on Hastings . . . [*Calling*] Pussy—pussy—puss. The question is—and I'd like your advice on this, Norman . . . [*He pauses, gazing up into the tree.*]

NORMAN: Look, could we cut this short? It's just I may have a divorce coming up next Tuesday and I'd hate to miss it. I don't want to rush you.

TOM: The point is, Norman, should I or should I not offer to go to Hastings too? I've been turning it over in my mind, should I or shouldn't I?

NORMAN: No.

TOM: Why is she going, I ask myself. Is she going as a gesture, a covert invitation aimed at me? Is she asking me to come with her, in fact?

NORMAN: No.

TOM: Is she saying, I'm going to Hastings. If you care about me at all, you must come to Hastings?

NORMAN: No.

TOM: Having first, of course, told me, in so many words, by a series of hints exactly where she was going.

NORMAN: Hastings.

TOM: Yes.

NORMAN: No. You've got the wrong end of the stick. If you want my opinion, that is subtle woman's language for stuff you, I'm off.

TOM: No. I don't see that. I think I'll have to have it out with her.

NORMAN: I wouldn't bother.

TOM: I'm giving that cat up for today. Coming in?

NORMAN: No, I'm going.

TOM: Oh. I thought you said you were staying.

NORMAN: No, I'm just passing through on my way to East Grinstead.

TOM: Really? Business?

NORMAN: Yes. International Association of Assistant Librarians Annual Conference.

TOM: Jolly good.

NORMAN: Exciting. [*Looking up in the tree*] Don't jump! Think of your wife and kittens.

TOM: Well, I'd better pop in.

[TOM *starts to move towards the house.* NORMAN *picks up his case.* REG *appears round the side of the house. He wears his cap and sports jacket and carries two suitcases.*]

REG: Oy—oy.

TOM: Ah!

NORMAN: Oh, no.

REG: Hallo, hallo. Who's this shifty looking pair?

TOM: Hallo there, Reg.

REG: Tom. [*He slaps him*] Norm. Surprise to see you. You're both looking good. Both looking good.

TOM: Yes . . . yes.

REG: What a day, eh? What a day. Ought to be knocking a ball about, eh? Well, that little lot took us— [*he checks his watch*] sixty two minutes exactly. Door to door. Know the trick? There's a trick to it. Don't take the A264. Take the A272 and then branch off onto the B2139. It looks longer but it isn't.

TOM: I usually take the A281.

NORMAN: Oh, my God.

REG: [*laughing*] How long does that take you?

TOM: About seventy-five minutes.

REG: Door to door?

TOM: Yes.

REG: Well, it would. You're going round the houses. If you want to go that way, you'd do better to go through East Grinstead.

NORMAN: [*jumping guiltily*] What, what?

REG: East Grinstead.

NORMAN: Oh.

TOM: Is Sarah here?

REG: Yes, yes. I think she went straight up to see Mother... [*Striding about*] Well, look at this for a day. What about this sunshine? Just the ticket. [*Spotting something in the tree*] Hallo, hallo. Anyone here a bird watcher?

NORMAN: Uh?

REG: Bird watcher, are you? Like watching birds? [*He laughs*] What do you make of that? Eh? You're a vet. What do you make of that?

TOM: Yes.

NORMAN: Good gracious, it's a cat.

REG: Cat. [*He laughs*] See it? Cat.

TOM: Silly creature.

REG: Mother's cat, isn't it?

TOM: Yes.

REG: Oh. Before I forget. Got another vet joke for you.

TOM: Oh yes.

REG: Question: What happens when a vet walks through a very deep puddle? Answer: He gets vater in his vellingtons.

TOM: Ha!

REG: Vater in his vellingtons. Heard that the other day. Tickled me.

NORMAN: Ha!

REG: What brings you here today, Norman? I didn't expect to see you. Ruth with you?

NORMAN: No.

REG: Thank goodness for that. No offence but thank goodness for that.

TOM: He's passing through.

NORMAN: Just passing through.

REG: Really?

TOM: Going to East Grinstead.

REG: Ah, now. From here? You'll be going from here?

NORMAN: Well, since this is where I am, it seems a good place to start.

REG: Turn left out of here—not right—through the village, then take the right fork past the pub—brings you onto the A272. Save you ten miles.

NORMAN: No, I don't fancy that way.

REG: Why not?

NORMAN: I haven't got a car.

REG: Ah, well. Catch the bus.

NORMAN: I'll do that.

[TOM *wanders to the house.*]

REG: Where are you going?

TOM: Just in.

REG: Try and persuade that wife of mine to put the kettle on.

TOM: Ah.

[TOM *goes in.*]

NORMAN: How is she?

REG: Who?

NORMAN: That wife of yours.

REG: I don't know. She's all right. When I last looked at her. [*He laughs.*] Well now, what's going on?

NORMAN: Eh?

REG: She off with Tom? Our Annie? Going off for a sly one with Tom?

NORMAN: Is she?

REG: Obvious. As soon as she wrote to Sarah—asked us to come and look after Mother for the weekend—I thought, hallo, what's up?

NORMAN: And Sarah?

REG: Sarah?

NORMAN: What did she think?

REG: No idea. Didn't ask her. No, she's off with Tom. You

could tell he was a bit on edge. Looked guilty. He must
have been desperate.

NORMAN: What do you mean, desperate?

REG: I mean. Knowing him. Not exactly one for taking the
plunge is he? Been hanging around here for, what, three
years? And I bet you they haven't got further than a
fumble on the sofa. Well, I'm glad. Glad for Annie. She's
a bright girl. Not a great beauty but her heart's in the
right place. Easy temperament, good around the house
. . .

NORMAN: All mod. cons, sunny view facing due south.

REG: What?

NORMAN: You talk as if she's a property up for sale.

REG: No. No. All I'm saying—

NORMAN: Better check her over for woodworm while
you're at it.

REG: [*laughing*] Check her over for woodworm, I like that.
[*Producing a bag from his pocket*] Want a toffee?

NORMAN: Not at the moment.

REG: [*having one*] What takes you to East Grinstead, then?

NORMAN: Oh—business.

REG: Business?

NORMAN: In a way.

REG: Oh yes?

NORMAN: [*winking*] Yes.

REG: [*laughing, knowingly*] Something lined up?

NORMAN: You might say that.

REG: Bit of stuff?

NORMAN: Just a little bit . . .

REG: Lucky chap. Hasn't got a friend has she?

NORMAN: She's got a sister, but she's married.

REG: Oh, well. I'm not fussy. You're on.

NORMAN: Reckon you'd get past Sarah?

REG: Ah. Well. Not seriously, no. I was only joking. I
would never . . . Don't believe in that personally. Mind
you, I've been tempted. When you've been married a
few years . . . you can't help window shopping. You

know, the old urge. But you keep it under control, don't you? You have to. Well, you may not have to. But I have to. Not that there isn't something to be said for it. I've often thought it might actually help a marriage sometimes. It gets a bit stale between you, you know. I'm not thinking just for me. For her too. Sarah. I'm not being selfish. Perhaps if she—went off for a few days with someone—she might—well, it might make her a bit more . . . you know, give her a fresh . . . get her going again, for God's sake. If you follow me.

NORMAN: Ah.

REG: Mind you, it'd never work for us. Sarah would never dream of going off. Pity. If she did, I could. But we're not like you and Ruth, you see.

NORMAN: What are we like?

REG: Well—easier—

NORMAN: There's nothing very easy about Ruth.

REG: No, I didn't mean easy like that, I meant—well, let's face it—you've always had, what shall we say—an unconventional relationship. Ruth was always a nonconformist you know. Even when we were kids. I envy those types, sometimes. Mother was another, you know. In a different way. That old lady up there's had a life, I can tell you.

NORMAN: I know.

REG: Wouldn't think so now. But she led our father a dance. Poor man really wasn't up to it. Shut himself in up there —pretended it all wasn't happening. Of course it was. Under his own roof sometimes. Well, it was bound to have an effect. Not so much on me—I was the eldest. Don't know what it did to Annie. She was younger. Think she just let it drift over her. Like she does now, most of the time. But Ruth. Ruth was altogether different.

NORMAN: I know, I live with her.

REG: She took it—oddly.

NORMAN: She's a mess.

REG: Putting it bluntly. She's got Mother's looks, mind

you. Attractive, wouldn't you say? Difficult for a brother
but—striking?

NORMAN: Oh, yes.

REG: Annie and I always said she had our share as well.
Certainly had mine. I don't think Sarah married me for
my looks.

NORMAN: I wonder why she did?

REG: I don't know. That's a good question. I must ask her
that sometime. [*He gets up*] Well, get going. She'll be
looking for me. [*He picks up his suitcases.*] Have a good trip.
Think of me—

NORMAN: I will.

REG: [*moving to the house, feeling the weight of his suitcase*]What
the hell's she put in this one? Must have packed the
bloody china cabinet. [*Turning back to* NORMAN] And
another thing. We've got children. You haven't. That
makes a difference. Can't go gallivanting off—not with
children. Responsibilities. Blast it.

[SARAH *comes out. Smartly dressed in her summer best.*]

SARAH: Reg—oh. [*She sees* NORMAN] Hallo, Norman.

NORMAN: Hallo, Sarah. How's Sarah?

SARAH: Very well, Norman. Surprised to hear you were
here.

NORMAN: Yes. Well, I was passing.

SARAH: That's nice.

NORMAN: Yes. Thought I'd look in on the old home.

SARAH: Naturally.

NORMAN: [*uneasy at her manner*] Well, I must be off. [*He
gathers himself together and picks up his case, preparing to leave.*]

SARAH: Are you taking those in, Reg?

REG: Oh, yes. Yes— [*He starts to move in.*]

SARAH: I've just been talking to Annie.

NORMAN: [*freezing in his tracks, warily*] Have you?

SARAH: Yes. Oh, Reg, rather good news. She's decided she
doesn't want to go away, after all.

REG: She doesn't?

NORMAN: Eh?

SARAH: No. Isn't that nice?

REG: Well, we needn't have bothered to come then.

SARAH: I think it's just as well we did.

REG: [*going in*] All this racing about and we didn't need to come at all.

[REG *goes inside.*]

SARAH: [*following him*] It gets difficult for her, coping entirely on her own . . . [*Turning back and smiling brilliantly at* NORMAN] Bye bye, Norman. I expect you'll want to hurry along to East Grinstead.

[SARAH *goes inside.* NORMAN *stands speechless with fury. He puts down his suitcase and paces up and down in silence for a second.*]

NORMAN: [*exploding with a fierce yell and kicking his suitcase frenziedly*] Damned—stupid—interfering—rotten—bitch.

[REG *comes out to fetch the bag he's left behind.*]

REG: Are you dashing off immediately or can you stay for a bit?

NORMAN: I'm staying. You bet your sweet life I'm staying.

[*He snatches up his suitcase and strides angrily into the house.* REG, *a little bewildered, follows him.*]

Curtain

ACT ONE

Scene Two

The garden. Saturday 9 p.m. SARAH *and* REG *come out from the house. They are supporting* NORMAN *who is very drunk.*

SARAH: All right, put him here. Put him here . . .

REG: [*lowering* NORMAN] Right. Down you come—

NORMAN: Thank you very much. Much obliged.

REG: Bit of fresh air should sober him up.

SARAH: I have never known anyone who can ruin an evening as thoroughly as he can.

NORMAN: Nobody loves me.

SARAH: Norman . . .

NORMAN: Nobody loves me at all.

REG: Shouldn't think so.

SARAH: Norman! Norman, listen to me . . . will you stop feeling sorry for yourself. Anything that's happened to you is entirely your own fault.

REG: It's the fault of that home-made wine, if you ask me.

SARAH: Reg . . .

REG: What?

SARAH: Would you mind leaving us for a moment and doing something useful?

REG: What?

SARAH: I don't know. Go and talk to Tom.

REG: Tom's gone home.

SARAH: Well, you could wash up the supper things. That wouldn't hurt you for once.

REG: Annie's doing that, isn't she? She doesn't want me.

SARAH: Annie is seeing to Mother. Anyway, we're supposed to be down here in order to give Annie a rest.

REG: We're supposed to have come down here in order that she can go away.

SARAH: Well, she obviously isn't going away, is she? Not with this one.

REG: I don't know why you didn't let them instead of interfering.

SARAH: Do you honestly believe it was me that stopped them going? Do you think I could have stopped them for a minute if they'd really wanted to go? If Annie had really wanted to go?

REG: I think you'd have had a good try. All right, I'll do the washing up.

SARAH: And put an apron on first otherwise you'll ruin those trousers.

REG: You know, I wouldn't have missed this weekend for anything in the world . . .

[REG goes in.]

SARAH: Norman . . .

NORMAN: Sarah, we're alone at last.

SARAH: Norman.

NORMAN: Mmm?

SARAH: I think it's about time we had a talk.

NORMAN: Oh no . . . don't bother, honestly Sarah. I'll just curl up here in the garden. I won't be any more trouble, I promise you.

SARAH: Norman.

NORMAN: What?

SARAH: Are you listening to me?

NORMAN: Yes, yes . . .

SARAH: I've no wish to waste my time with you if you're not going to listen to me. I've a dozen things I could be doing at home. I've got two children to worry about, a house, a husband—of sorts. But the point is I seem to be the only one in this family capable of making any sort of decision at all. I mean whether or not I like it, I seem to be the head of this family at the moment. By rights, it ought to be Reg . . . if you've lived with Reg, you know he can't even pay a gas bill. How he's still an estate agent after all these years I never cease to wonder. I'm amazed he hasn't sold someone the same house twice . . .

NORMAN: What's wrong with that? That's standard estate agent's practice, isn't it?

SARAH: Did you stop for a minute and seriously think of what you were doing when you asked Annie away this weekend? Did you ever think what the consequences might be?

NORMAN: Ruth wouldn't care. She doesn't care.

SARAH: I'm not worried about you and Ruth, you—well, what you do is your business—I'm thinking of Annie. What about her?

NORMAN: She'd have had a good weekend. I'd have given her that. What have you ever given her? What's anyone ever given her?

SARAH: Very noble of you . . .

NORMAN: Not noble. She'd have probably given me a good weekend.

SARAH: And what would have happened to her and Tom?

NORMAN: He'd never have known.

SARAH: He'd have found out.

NORMAN: Meaning you would have told him?

SARAH: No. Annie would have done.

NORMAN: Annie? She's not that stupid . . .

SARAH: She's in love with him.

NORMAN: With Tom?

SARAH: Yes.

NORMAN: Rubbish. You. You've seen them together. She kicks him round the place like an old football. A punctured football. He doesn't even bounce back.

SARAH: If she kicks him, it's probably the only way she can get any reaction from him at all. What else is a woman supposed to do if she's stuck with a man like that?

NORMAN: Tom doesn't love anybody. Except cats and bull terriers . . . she's damn lucky he's so even tempered. I told him—the way she treats him—he ought to take a swing at her.

SARAH: I'm sure she'd prefer that to being ignored.

NORMAN: She doesn't want Tom . . . stop trying to push everybody together, that cat's still up there. [*Calling*] Puss, puss, puss. He's gone now. You can come down . . . [*To* SARAH] Present company excepted, the trouble with the men in this house—and I include your husband—is they allow themselves to be trampled on by the giant feet of their cow elephant spouses.

SARAH: Whose fault is that?

NORMAN: Just because Reg happens to be a very gentle, friendly soul . . . just because Tom happens to be a man who's never had an aggressive thought in his little head, in his little life, doesn't mean it's a cue for every woman in sight to bounce up and down on them like nubile lady trampoline artists . . . what have you done to him? Look at him, in there, little Reg in his pinny, busy with his little bridget brush polishing away. Polishing the plates for dear life because Sarah said so.

SARAH: While you're lying out here stinking of drink.

NORMAN: That's a man's role. To lie about stinking of drink.

SARAH: I bet you've never washed up in your life.

NORMAN: I line up the dishes and smash them—slowly—with the steak tenderizer . . . remind me, I'll give Reg one for Christmas. That'd give you something to complain about.

SARAH: You really don't understand me at all, do you? You don't like me and you've never tried to understand me . . .

NORMAN: I understand you.

SARAH: But you don't like me? Do you?

NORMAN: I—don't dislike you. You're like—mild athlete's foot. You make me irritable.

SARAH: I see.

NORMAN: I'll tell you. When I was at my Primary school—

mixed infants—we had a little girl just like you. She was
very pretty, very smart and clean—beautifully dressed—
always a nicely starched little frock on—nicely ironed
bow in her hair . . . butter wouldn't melt anywhere. Let
alone her mouth. And she ran that little school with more
sheer ruthless efficiency than the head of the Mafia. She
asked you to do something for her and you did it. You
never argued. It was no good arguing with her. She was
cleverer than you were. Precociously clever. She could
reduce a nine year old thug to tears with her sarcasm.
And it was no use trying to thump her either. She'd se-
duced all the best muscle in the place. She had a body
guard five deep. Not that she ever needed it. For some
reason, she took a real dislike to me. Maybe because she
could see what I really thought of her. She made my life
murder. I was terrified to go to school. I used to pretend
to be sick—I used to hide—play truant—anything rather
than go . . . And then one day, in the holidays, she came
round with her mother to our house to see my mother. A
sociable tea and chat. And they sent us two out on our
own to play together. And suddenly there we were, not
in the school, not in the playground—which was definitely her territory—but on mine. My garden, my patch.
And we stood there and we just looked at each other. And
I thought what am I frightened of you for? A skinny little
girl with knock knees and a front tooth missing—what on
earth have I been frightened of you for, for heaven's sake?
So I picked her up, like this under one arm and I carried
her right down the bottom of the garden by the rubbish
tip—she never made a sound during this, not a word,
nothing—and I found the biggest patch of stinging nettles
I could find and I pulled down her knickers and sat her
right in the middle of them. I felt marvellous. It was a
beautiful moment. Magic. And she sat there for a very
long time—not moving, just looking at me—weighing me
up, you know. Then she got up, pulled up her knickers,
very quietly took hold of my hand, gave me a big kiss and

we went in and had our tea. I've never been in love like that again.

SARAH: I don't believe a word of that.

NORMAN: It may have been an allegory.

SARAH: Really? Meaning what?

NORMAN: Meaning watch it. This garden's full of nettles.

SARAH: I believe you would, too. If you weren't so drunk.

NORMAN: I would if I thought you'd give me a kiss . . . [*He reaches out and touches her hand.*]

SARAH: [*without moving her hand away*] Oh, Norman. Ruth, then Annie, then me. Be your age.

NORMAN: [*taking her hand more firmly*] I don't mean any harm . . .

SARAH: You're so dopey, I don't know how anybody could fall for you.

NORMAN: God knows. [*He kisses her hand*] Animal magnetism.

SARAH: You've no morals. No nothing, have you?

NORMAN: I'm full of love.

SARAH: And wine . . .

NORMAN: [*moving closer*] By God, you're lovely.

SARAH: [*snatching away her arm*] Now, Norman. That's enough . . .

NORMAN: [*kneeling up by her*] Going to call Reg, are you?

SARAH: [*remaining where she is*] That's enough . . .
[NORMAN *kisses her swiftly.*]
Enough . . .

NORMAN: [*softly*] Help, help, Reg . . .

SARAH: That's enough, I said. [*She kisses him*] Quite enough—[*She kisses him*] No more . . .

NORMAN: Sorry.

SARAH: Enough. [*She kisses him again. This time it develops into a long kiss. Passionately*] Oh my God, what am I doing . . .

NORMAN: [*kissing her all over*] I know what you're doing. Don't worry. I'll tell you later.

SARAH: [*struggling free*] Norman . . . Norman . . . I'll get you something to eat, Norman.

NORMAN: [*persistent*] I've got you—that's enough . . .

SARAH: [*still struggling*] No—please—Norman—please . . . let me get you something to eat—and then I'll come back . . . Norman. [*She pulls away finally.*]

NORMAN: Where are you going, Sarah?

SARAH: [*breathless*] I want to get you something to eat. I want you to eat something . . . please let me get you something to eat. I'll come back.

NORMAN: Come back . . .

SARAH: As soon as I've got you something . . .
[ANNIE *has come out of the house. A silence.*]

ANNIE: Oh, I'm sorry. Were you having a private conversation?

SARAH: [*in some disarray*] No—no. I was just getting Norman something to eat . . .
[SARAH *goes inside.*]

ANNIE: What's the matter with her?

NORMAN: How do you mean?

ANNIE: Well, she's all—jittery.

NORMAN: No.

ANNIE: Have you two been getting at each other again?

NORMAN: Well . . . here and there.

ANNIE: You've never got on with her, have you? I know she's difficult. I mean, she drives me up the wall sometimes . . . but honestly, Norman, if you can just try and be nice to her—it does pay off.

NORMAN: I'll bear it in mind.

ANNIE: Look at you, you old tip . . . [*She kicks him.*]

NORMAN: Don't do that.

ANNIE: Lovely night. I had to read to Mother. She wouldn't go off to sleep for ages. I wouldn't mind but she likes these awful books.

NORMAN: What sort? Horror stories, knowing her.

ANNIE: They wouldn't be so bad. I don't object to horror stories. No, she insists on all these torrid romances. I mean really. It's bad enough having to buy them with their incredible front covers—I have to wrap them round with copies of Country Life to carry them home. But then having to read them out loud . . . it's awfully embarrassing. And you can't skip anything. Come on, she says, come on they did more than that, come on.

NORMAN: She's an evil lady, that one. No wonder you're all peculiar.

ANNIE: Norman.

NORMAN: Uh?

ANNIE: Look, I know why you got drunk tonight . . .

NORMAN: Oh. You've guessed my secret.

ANNIE: It was because I let you down, wasn't it?

NORMAN: Good Lord, no.

ANNIE: I feel really dreadful.

NORMAN: Think nothing of it.

ANNIE: The worst thing is, we planned the weekend in January—we talked and wrote about it for six months—and you go ahead and get it all organized and—well, I don't think I really could have gone anyway. It was just a dream. Something you think about but never really mean to do. And then you turn up here and—

NORMAN: The dream's shattered.

ANNIE: What I'm saying is, don't blame Sarah. She merely said what I was feeling. You mustn't take it out on her. You mustn't hate her.

NORMAN: Right.

ANNIE: It's my fault. I'm a coward.

NORMAN: Forget it.

ANNIE: Tom was awfully odd this evening. I don't think he knows, but I think he suspects. He was almost rude for Tom. Told me I looked like an old Post Office sack or something.

NORMAN: Good God, the man's a sadist.

ANNIE: I suppose I do a bit. I think I'm going to make one of my efforts tomorrow. I haven't made an effort for a bit.

NORMAN: You're fine.

ANNIE: Norman, look. I'm going to say something. But
you're not to look at me while I'm saying it . . . do you
promise?

NORMAN: What do you intend to do while you're saying it,
may I ask?

ANNIE: Nothing. It's just I'll get embarrassed if you do . . .

NORMAN: You're going to read me one of Mother's books,
aren't you?

ANNIE: Oh, Norman. This is frightfully difficult. Please . . .

NORMAN: Sorry. Won't look . . .

ANNIE: I promised you this weekend. I promised I'd go
away with you and that I'd stay with you in a hotel and
—everything . . . well, I've let you down. I've been a
coward.

NORMAN: No, no . . .

ANNIE: I think the bit that made me a coward was the
going away bit really. The actual thing of going into a
hotel. All that pretending. It just isn't really me. I'd just
get embarrassing and stupid.

NORMAN: Never.

ANNIE: Anyway. I'm not a coward about anything else . . .
do you get what I mean?

NORMAN: No.

ANNIE: Oh, for heaven's sake . . . if you want to come to
my room tonight, you'll be very welcome, that's all. You
can look now.

[NORMAN *looks. A pause.*]
Well?

NORMAN: Well.

ANNIE: I suppose I've done that all wrong too.

NORMAN: Not at all. Not at all.

[*Pause.*]

ANNIE: Well. Say something. Even if it's only thank you.

NORMAN: Er—what time?

ANNIE: What?

NORMAN: Would you like me to come? What time would
you like me to come?

ANNIE: Well—when you like—I don't know. Don't make it too late, I'll be asleep.

NORMAN: Right. It's just I've got one or two things to do first . . .

ANNIE: Suit yourself. I'm going up to make up your bed. Just for appearances, I should get into it and make it look used. You know—

NORMAN: Good point, yes.

ANNIE: Just for Sarah's benefit.

NORMAN: What?

ANNIE: In case she . . .

NORMAN: Yes, right. I'll mess it up for Sarah.

ANNIE: [*kissing him lightly*] See you later then?

NORMAN: Right.

[REG *has appeared in an apron, holding a salad basket.*]

REG: [*seeing them*] Oh. Beg your pardon, beg your pardon . . .

ANNIE: What for?

REG: [*winking*] Sorry, sorry. I saw nothing. Nothing at all. Don't worry . . . [*Holding up salad basket*] Sarah says, where does this go?

ANNIE: I don't know. Just sling it on top of the cupboard. That's what I do.

REG: Oh, right . . .

ANNIE: [*taking it from him*] It's all right. I'll do it, I'm going in. Anyway, you've got to know how to sling it . . .

[ANNIE *goes indoors.*]

REG: Hallo there, Norman.

NORMAN: Hallo there, Reg. You come to seduce me?

REG: Eh?

NORMAN: Nothing.

REG: Ah. That's done that, anyway. I hate washing up. Look at these hands. Ruined. [*He laughs.*] Hey, I'm going to get myself a drink. Do you want one?

NORMAN: Great.

REG: Think we've earned one.

NORMAN: Bring the bottle.

REG: Right.

[REG *goes in.*]

NORMAN: This boy can do no wrong tonight. He has the Midas touch. Every woman turns to gold. [*Shouting at the cat*] Come down here, cat. You don't know what you're missing.

[REG *reappears.*]

REG: Who are you shouting at?

[NORMAN *points.*]

Oh, yes. Hallo, pussy. Here we are.

[NORMAN *takes the bottle from him.* REG *holds out two glasses.* NORMAN *fills one and wanders away with the bottle.*]

Don't you want a glass?

NORMAN: I'll drink from the bottle. I'm all man tonight.

REG: [*sitting*] Wish I was. I'm clapped out. Cheers. [*He drinks.*]

NORMAN: Good health, Reg. [*He swigs.*] Ah, it's a good night, Reg. It's a lovely night.

REG: Beautiful . . .

NORMAN: It's on a night such as this that all the old base instincts of primitive man, the hunter, come flooding up. You long to be away—free—filled with the urge to rape and pillage and conquer.

REG: I've just got the urge to put my feet up. I think my ankles are swelling again.

NORMAN: My God! I'm filled with the lust for conquest tonight.

REG: [*examining his legs*] I'm going to get varicose veins if I'm not careful. That'll be the next thing. I've just about got everything else . . .

NORMAN: [*excitedly*] Reg, I have this tremendous idea. I want to tell you about this tremendous idea, Reg. May I tell you about my tremendous idea?

REG: All right, yes, if you want to . . .

NORMAN: It's suddenly come to me, this tremendous idea. It's terrific. Let's all of us—you, me, Tom—let's take a couple of weeks and just go . . .

REG: Go? Where?

NORMAN: Anywhere. Just we men . . .

REG: Do you mean a holiday?

NORMAN: Well, in a way—no, not a holiday—that sounds so damn conventional. I want us just to go . . . And see things. And taste things. And smell things. And touch things . . . touch trees—and grass—and—and earth. Let's touch earth together, Reg.

REG: Where were you thinking of going?

NORMAN: Everywhere. Let's see everywhere. Let's be able to say—we have seen and experienced everything.

REG: We'd have to be going some to do that in two weeks, wouldn't we?

NORMAN: I've never really looked before, you know, Reg. These kids today, you know, they've got the right ideas. This world is my world and I'm going to wrap my arms right round it and hug it to me.

REG: I'd go easy on that stuff, you know . . .

NORMAN: In one great big bloody beautiful embrace.

REG: Yes. Ssh, now quietly, Norman. Mother's asleep.

NORMAN: When you think of the things we've done with our lives—our little lives up to this moment—you realize—what a waste. What a dreadful waste. [*To the heavens*] Please don't let me die till I've seen it. Please don't let me die.

REG: [*rising anxiously*] It's all right, Norman. You're not going to die, it's all right.

NORMAN: [*turning and embracing* REG] Oh, Reg . . .

REG: Ssh. Steady on. Steady on. Quietly . . .

NORMAN: [*tearful*] You're my brother, Reg, my brother.

REG: Yes, well, brother-in-law, yes. [*He tries to disentangle himself.*] Look, Norman . . .

NORMAN: Let's stop hating and start to love, Reg.

REG: Ssh. Yes, yes—good idea . . .

NORMAN: I love you, Reg. I'm not ashamed to say that to my brother. I love you.

REG: That's good news, Norman, yes.

[SARAH *enters with a plate of sandwiches. She stops as she sees the men.* ANNIE, *alarmed by the noise, enters separately behind her, pillow case in hand.*]

NORMAN: I love you, Reg, I love you.

[NORMAN *collapses clasping* REG'S *knees.* REG *looks at the women.* ANNIE *and* SARAH *looks at each other, then back at* REG.]

REG: He's—er—he's obviously had a—he's had a—he's [*he pauses*]

SARAH: We'd better get him inside.

REG: Yes.

[SARAH *puts down her plate. They gather round* NORMAN *preparing to drag him inside.* NORMAN *starts sobbing.*]
He's crying.

SARAH: He's drunk. That's all he is, drunk. Come on, we'll have to pull him. I'm not lifting him. Come on—pull . . .
[*They start to haul* NORMAN *indoors by his arms.*]

NORMAN: [*tearfully as he goes*] Nobody loves me . . . nobody loves me . . . nobody loves me at all . . .

Curtain

ACT TWO

SCENE ONE

The garden. 11 a.m. Sunday morning. RUTH *is standing thoughtfully.* SARAH *has just come out carrying two slightly ancient collapsible garden chairs.*

RUTH: Well.

SARAH: Yes.

RUTH: Norman and Annie. Well, well.

SARAH: Yes. I thought you ought to know.

RUTH: Thank you for phoning me. I don't know what I'm expected to do though.

SARAH: Well . . .

RUTH: I mean, one can't take it very seriously. It's obviously only another of Norman's gestures against the world or me or whatever. It's not as if they've even done anything.

SARAH: I think you might've done a little more than just laugh. I mean, if I'd been in your position I certainly would have . . .

RUTH: Sarah, dear, I've been married to Norman for five years. I have learnt through bitter experience that the last thing to do with Norman is to take him seriously. That's exactly what he wants. I'm not saying it isn't a strain sometimes—to keep smiling when he's behaving particularly bizarrely and threatening to burn down the house . . . When he really gets on top of me, I just go to bed and lock the door.

SARAH: I'm amazed you've stayed with him, I really am.

RUTH: Well, I don't really look at it that way. I rather think of him as staying with me. After all, I make all the payments on the house, most of the furniture is mine . . . it has crossed my mind, in moments of extreme provocation, to throw him out . . . but, I don't know, I think I must be rather fond of him. It's a bit like owning an oversized unmanageable dog, being married to Norman. He's not very well house-trained, he needs continual exercising— mental and physical—and it's sensible to lock him up if you have visitors. Otherwise he mauls them. But I'd hate to get rid of him.

SARAH: That's all very well if you keep him under proper control. When he goes upsetting other people's lives. Annie's for example . . .

RUTH: You really can't blame Norman entirely, you know. He only jumps up at people who encourage him. It's a general rule, if you don't want him licking your face, don't offer him little titbits . . . I don't mean just Annie either.

SARAH: I don't know what you're talking about.

RUTH: Oh, come on Sarah, I'm sure at some time he's cast an eye in your direction.

SARAH: Certainly not.

RUTH: In fact I've seen him do it.

SARAH: Rubbish. Don't assume everyone's motives are the same as your own. Anyway, the point is, so far as I can gather, Annie and Tom are practically not on speaking terms. They had words, apparently, last night. I don't think he knows about Norman, but all the same, Tom senses something. He's very upset.

RUTH: Oh, she's not still with that limp man . . .

SARAH: Tom would make her a very good husband. I mean he may have his faults but when you compare him to some men . . . he's kind, very considerate. He's done a lot for Annie over the years . . .

RUTH: He's as selfish as hell.

SARAH: That is just not true . . .

RUTH: He is quite content, from all accounts, to come round here day after day, eat her food, use the place as a second home—come and go just as he pleases and what's he given her in return? Absolutely nothing.

SARAH: I think that's extremely unfair.

RUTH: He's a parasite. Like one of the tics on his wretched animals.

SARAH: Oh well, it's obviously not worth discussing this with you. We don't see eye to eye on anything. We never have.

RUTH: [*taking one of the chairs and starting to put it up*] Quite right. Very sensible. I'm going to enjoy a bit of sun. Then I'm going home to do some work. It was very kind of you to phone me and express so much concern over my relationship with Norman. As I say, there's nothing I can do about it. Norman is a law unto himself and always has been and I have a mountain of work to do by tomorrow. What the hell's wrong with this chair? [*She struggles to put it up.*]

SARAH: If you'd wear your glasses it would help.

RUTH: Oh, don't you start on me about my glasses. Norman's bad enough.

SARAH: You grope about—drive cars . . .

RUTH: Look, go away Sarah. You're a pain in the neck.

SARAH: I think Norman's just about what you deserve, I really do . . .

RUTH: [*still grappling*] Damn and blast this thing . . .

SARAH: Here, come on, let me . . .

RUTH: [*fiercely*] Oh, go away.

SARAH: All right, all right. I still don't know why you don't wear your glasses. They're a great improvement.

[SARAH *goes in.* RUTH *glares after her. She has one final go at the chair, gives up and, putting it on its side, sits on it this way, rather uncomfortably.* TOM *wanders on.*]

TOM: Oh. Ruth. Hallo.

RUTH: Who's that? Oh . . . hallo.

TOM: You're here?

RUTH: Yes.

TOM: Ah.

[TOM *notices the way* RUTH *is sitting on her chair. He studies her for a moment, puzzled.*]

Er . . .

RUTH: What?

TOM: Nothing. I—er . . . [*Gesturing vaguely towards her chair*] Nothing.

[TOM *selects the other chair, is about to put it up then decides, perhaps out of courtesy, to sit on it the same as* RUTH *is doing on hers.*]

Seen Norman?

RUTH: Yes.

TOM: Ah. Seen Annie?

RUTH: Yes.

TOM: Ah. [*Pause.*]

RUTH: I've also seen Reg and Sarah . . . in fact, I think I've seen just about everybody there is to see.

TOM: Ah. Now you've seen me.

RUTH: Yes. I've seen you.

TOM: You look—different. Can't think why. Different.

RUTH: I'm older, perhaps.

TOM: No, no . . . can't think. It'll come to me. [*Pause.*] Er . . .

RUTH: What?

TOM: I was just wondering if there was any reason why we were sitting like this.

RUTH: I don't know why you should be.

TOM: No, nor do I.

RUTH: I know why I am.

TOM: Oh? Why?

RUTH: Because I can't put the bloody thing up.

TOM: [*leaping into action*] Oh. Well. Just a sec. Excuse me. Hang on. [*He puts the chair up*] Here we are.

RUTH: Thank you.

[*They both sit.*]

TOM: You've seen Annie, you say?

RUTH: Yes.

TOM: Ah. How did she look?

RUTH: Aren't you going to put your chair up?

TOM: Oh yes. Good idea.

[TOM *puts up his chair and sits.*]

RUTH: Annie looks very well. From what I've seen.

TOM: The point is—I think I'm in her bad books.

RUTH: Really?

TOM: Yes. I rather went at her last night. Tore her off a strip.

RUTH: You did?

TOM: Yes, I thought it might—well, she seemed to be taking me far too much for granted.

RUTH: Was she?

TOM: So I thought a couple of sharp words might do the trick. I told her to straighten herself up.

RUTH: Did you?

TOM: Told her she looked a mess.

RUTH: Really?

TOM: Yes. I threatened to belt her. Really let rip.

RUTH: I see.

TOM: I haven't slept a wink. Do you think I've damaged my chances?

RUTH: Chances of what?

TOM: I don't know. Just general chances.

RUTH: Well. Some women do respond awfully well to that sort of treatment. They enjoy tremendously being told they look a mess—and they actually thrill to the threat of physical violence. I've never met one that does, mind you, but they probably do exist. In books. By men. But then, there are probably some women who enjoy being thrown into canals. One just doesn't bump into them every day —not even in this family.

TOM: You reckon I might possibly have been on the wrong track?

RUTH: I'd have thought so.

TOM: Oh, well. For once he was wrong.

RUTH: Who was wrong?

TOM: Norman.

RUTH: Norman? Did Norman tell you to do that?

TOM: He suggested I do something of the sort.

RUTH: Insult her and threaten to beat her up?

TOM: Yes. He's generally right. About women, anyway. He's got a good instinct, has Norman. Has a way with women. I shouldn't really be saying this, should I?

RUTH: [*after looking at* TOM *for a while incredulously*] Tom.

TOM: Um?

RUTH: At the risk of pouring bad advice on bad, I think perhaps I ought to point you in the right direction . . .

TOM: Do. Yes, do. Any advice . . .

RUTH: Firstly, there are fallacies in Norman's well-known universal theory of womanhood with which, as it happens, as his wife, I am familiar. He claims that women can be divided into two groups—the ones you stroke and the ones you swipe. There has been some research done on this and it's been discovered quite recently that they are actually a little more complex.

TOM: Yes, yes. It follows . . .

RUTH: Good. They enjoy flattery no less than a man does. Though if you are flattering a woman, it pays to be a little more subtle. You don't have to bother with men, they believe any compliment automatically . . .

TOM: Oh, come on. Hardly, hardly . . .

RUTH: Well, we won't argue that. All I'm saying is, Tom, you're an intelligent man, you're not unattractive . . .

TOM: Oh well, thank you very much.

RUTH: And you obviously feel a lot of things that you don't show—necessarily. Which is marvellous in a crisis but a bit disheartening in times of peace.

TOM: How do you mean?

RUTH: I think you have to give a little. Give, Tom, do you see?

TOM: Ah.

RUTH: Do you follow me?

TOM: [*comprehending*] Aha—yes. [*He sits back and ponders this.*] Give a little what?

RUTH: Oh, my God. [*She rises impatiently*] You're a very

frustrating person to talk to, Tom. I feel like a tame mouse on one of those wheels they have in cages—one keeps running round and round like mad getting nowhere.

TOM: That's interesting you should mention that. There have been some studies done. Mice and wheels and it's really quite remarkable. One of the things they discovered—

RUTH: Yes, right. Thank you.

TOM: Eh?

RUTH: Don't let's wander off the subject.

TOM: No.

RUTH: [*studying him*] I think your brain works all right. I think what must happen is, it receives a message from outside—but once that message gets inside your head, it must be like an unfiled internal memo in a vast civil service department. It gets shunted from desk to desk with nobody willing to take responsibility for it. Let's try some simple reactions shall we? I hate you, Tom. Do you hear? I hate you.

TOM: Um?

RUTH: Oh well, try again. I love you, Tom. I love you . . .

TOM: [*laughing nervously*] I don't quite get this—a game, is it?

RUTH: No, Tom, it is not a game. It's an attempt to communicate.

TOM: Ah.

RUTH: You're refreshing after Norman, I'll give you that. Who is never one to hide anything. He has three emotions for every occasion.

TOM: I know what it is. Why you look different. You're not wearing your glasses.

RUTH: No.

TOM: Makes a great difference to you, that. Without your glasses.

RUTH: Thank you, Tom. That's good. You're learning.

TOM: I think I prefer you with them on, actually. It gives your face a better shape. [*Gesturing vaguely*] Sort of . . .

RUTH: [*menacing*] Tom . . .

TOM: Um?

RUTH: Do you get on well with your animals, by any chance?

TOM: Yes, yes, generally . . .

RUTH: You amaze me. You have a disastrous effect on me, did you know that?

TOM: Oh.

RUTH: Everything tends to boil over ever so slightly.

TOM: Oh. It's pretty warm.

RUTH: I have a desire to put on my glasses and take off my clothes and dance naked on the grass for you, Tom. I'd put on my glasses not in order to improve the shape of my face, but in order to see your reaction, if any. And as I whirled faster and faster—the sun glinting on my lenses —flashing messages of passion and desire, I would hurl you to the ground, rip off your clothes and we would roll over and over making mad, torrid, steaming love together. How does that grab you, Tom?

TOM: [*after a moment*] Good Lord. [*He laughs.*] Have to be careful where you rolled on this grass.

RUTH: Oh. [*She sits exhausted, head in hands.*]

TOM: [*watching her anxiously*] Ruth? Are you all right? Fairly hot this sun. Nearly overhead. Perhaps you ought to have a lie down . . .

RUTH: I'm sorry. I'm exhausted. I've done my best. I'm sorry.

TOM: [*rising and flapping round her*] Can I get you an aspirin? [RUTH *lies back with her eyes closed.* TOM *moves about anxiously.*]

Look, I had no idea you felt like this. I honestly had no idea.

RUTH: Like what?

TOM: Like that. With me.

RUTH: [*through gritted teeth*] I have never hidden my feelings towards you, Tom.

TOM: I just thought of us as friends. Nothing more or less. I had no idea . . .

RUTH: What are you talking about, Tom?

TOM: I feel terrible about this. Absolutely terrible. This has complicated things no end. I mean, it looks as if the ball's in my court rather. Yes, you've bowled me a googly there.

RUTH: What the hell is a googly?

TOM: If a woman, unexpectedly, suddenly tells you she loves you, where do you go from there?

RUTH: Are we talking theoretically?

TOM: If you like.

RUTH: Well, it's rather up to you then, isn't it? Firstly, you have to ask yourself, do I love her?

TOM: Well, I haven't had much time to think. I mean, love's a bit strong. Anyway, there's somebody else.

RUTH: What are you talking about?

TOM: Well, there's Norman. I've got to think of Norman's feelings.

RUTH: Norman? Don't be so damned ridiculous. As far as Norman's concerned, this is some passing romantic pipe-dream. So stop using Norman as an excuse for your own inadequacy. If you don't grab quickly, somebody else will sooner or later. Someone with a little more determination than Norman ever had.

TOM: Well. I'm sorry. That's all I can say. I had no idea. Does Norman know, do you think?

RUTH: What?

TOM: About me?

RUTH: Of course he knows.

TOM: Oh, that explains it. That's why he's been a bit odd towards me. Slightly strained, you know. Oh well.
[*A pause.*]
You're looking very nice, by the way. Lovely. Very nice indeed. Very well turned out.

RUTH: I think you're a raving lunatic.

TOM: [*modestly*] Well, I go a bit over the moon, sometimes. You don't need to worry.

RUTH: I'm terrified to be left alone in the same county.

[ANNIE *comes out. She has made her effort. She has done her hair, made up a little and has a dress on.*]

TOM: Oh hallo.

ANNIE: Hallo. You both want some coffee out here?

TOM: Oh, well—

RUTH: [*getting up*] No. I've had enough sun. I think I'll go and brave Mother.

ANNIE: Yes, she's awake. I've just been in with her.

RUTH: Right. [*Passing close to* TOM] Talk to her.

TOM: Eh?

RUTH: Tell her.

TOM: Oh.

ANNIE: You want coffee, Tom?

TOM: No, that's all right. [*Studying* ANNIE] You know, you look different somehow. What is it?

RUTH: [*as she goes*] She probably hasn't got her glasses on. [RUTH *goes in.*]

TOM: No. It isn't that. It'll come to me.

ANNIE: Don't force it.

[*A pause.*]

Did you catch the cat?

TOM: Yes. He was round the front there, when I arrived. Sitting in the sun, purring away.

ANNIE: Good. Is his paw better?

TOM: Oh yes. It wasn't anything serious really—I—

ANNIE: The way you went on about it, I thought you were going to have to amputate a leg.

TOM: No, well—actually, you may not have noticed but you probably seem to have the unhealthiest cat in the country.

ANNIE: He hasn't had a day without something. He's either got feeble resistance or else he's a terrific hypochondriac. I don't know which. It's the only cat I know with a personal physician.

TOM: I'm afraid I do rather use him actually. As a reason for coming.

ANNIE: Well, there's no need. You're welcome any time.

It seems a bit unfair to keep pumping him full of medicine, just as an excuse for a meal.

TOM: I don't quite do that . . .

ANNIE: Well . . .

TOM: Yes.

ANNIE: Any time.

TOM: Thanks.

[*A pause.*]

ANNIE: Tom. I've got to tell you something.

TOM: Yes. So have I.

ANNIE: Yes, well let me tell you mine first. I think I know what you're going to say and this may make all the difference. The point is that this weekend Norman asked me to go away with him.

TOM: Norman?

ANNIE: Yes. He wanted us to go away together for a weekend. As you see we didn't go but—I thought you ought to know that we were considering it. I nearly agreed. There, I've said it. That's it.

TOM: [*slowly*] I see.

ANNIE: I'm sorry.

TOM: No—no—

ANNIE: Are you hurt?

TOM: Well—I understand—I think—

ANNIE: You do? You wouldn't have wanted me to go, would you?

TOM: No. But I don't think I'd have had the right to stop you.

ANNIE: Yes, well, maybe not—technically. I know we're not that close. All the same, I thought you might have felt—

TOM: No, it's not that. It's not you. It's just that I think I understand what Norman was doing.

ANNIE: He was asking me away to a hotel.

TOM: Yes, I know that. But why was he?

ANNIE: Why does any man?

TOM: Yes, yes, yes. But you see, behind all that, in some obscure way, I think he wanted to get back at me.

ANNIE: Get back at you?

TOM: He knows, you see.

ANNIE: Knows what?

TOM: About Ruth and me.

ANNIE: Ruth and you?

TOM: Yes. That's what I wanted to tell you.

ANNIE: You and Ruth?

TOM: Yes.

ANNIE: But you haven't—with Ruth—?

TOM: No. Not *with* Ruth, no.

ANNIE: Well, with who then?

TOM: No, it is with Ruth but not me with Ruth, rather Ruth with me. There's a difference.

ANNIE: Is there?

TOM: Yes. You see, it appears that Ruth—you'll have to bear with me, this is fraught with embarrassment—Ruth, you see—I'm so useless at this, I never pick up these signals and signs and hints till it's far too late. Ruth's apparently been carrying a torch for me.

ANNIE: She has?

TOM: I didn't encourage her, I promise you. As a matter of fact, I didn't even know. Till just now.

ANNIE: Are you sure you've got this right, Tom? Ruth can be a little—well, quick, you know. I mean, I'm not saying you did, but could you have missed the point?

TOM: No. I assure you, I did not miss the point. No chance of that. Rather wish I had. She made it all graphically clear. She wanted to take off her clothes—oh, well it's very embarrassing. I won't go into it.

ANNIE: No, go on. Take off her clothes?

TOM: Oh, well she went on, you know. I hate you, I love you—I want to roll about naked in my glasses . . .

ANNIE: Are you sure you got this right?

TOM: Yes. She said she'd never belonged to Norman. It was just a pipe-dream—that Norman knew all about it and I'd better grab her while she's still boiling over.

ANNIE: I don't believe it. What did you say?

TOM: I was a bit taken aback. I said I'd have to think it over.

ANNIE: [*indignant*] Think it over?

TOM: Obviously.

ANNIE: What about me?

TOM: Yes, well, that too . . .

ANNIE: Yes, that too . . .

TOM: Oh goodness, this is getting awfully difficult.

ANNIE: Not at all. It's not difficult. Don't let me stand in your way. You rush off.

TOM: No—no—

ANNIE: Go on. Go on. Good riddance.

TOM: No, Annie, I—

ANNIE: And in future I'd be grateful if you'd stop molesting our damn cat.

[REG *appears in shirt sleeves. He has a tennis ball with him.*]

REG: Right! Here we are. I've got the ball. Catch, Annie—
[*He throws the ball to* ANNIE.]

ANNIE: [*catching it through reflex*] Oh, Reg, not now . . . [*She throws the ball back.*]

REG: Come on, Come on. [*Calling indoors*] Norman! Come on out. We can all do with some exercise. Stuck indoors far too much.

ANNIE: Reg, please, not just at the . . .
[NORMAN *comes out. He wears shorts, a tee shirt and his woolly hat.*]

NORMAN: Right, where's the action then?

REG: What are you wearing?

NORMAN: Found them upstairs in the cupboard.

REG: I think they're my old ones.

NORMAN: Thank you for the loan. [*Seeing* ANNIE] Hey-hey! What is this, I see?

ANNIE: What?

NORMAN: Look at her. Just take a look at this beautiful girl.

REG: Oh yes. She's got a skirt on.

NORMAN: The sunshine has brought the butterfly out of its chrysalis. Isn't she beautiful?

ANNIE: All right Norman, don't overdo it.

NORMAN: No, honestly, you look great. Doesn't she, Tom?

TOM: That's what it is. You've got a thing on. A dress. I knew there was something different.

NORMAN: Give the boy a wolf cub badge. [*To* ANNIE] Fantastic.

ANNIE: Oh, shut up.

REG: Are we going to play a game?

NORMAN: Right.

ANNIE: No.

NORMAN: Oh come on. Don't get ladylike just because you're in drag.

REG: What are we playing?

NORMAN: I know. I've got it. Strip catch. Every time you drop the ball, you take something off. Here, Annie, catch. [*He mimes throwing the ball to her.* ANNIE *reacts*] Missed. Right, get 'em off.

ANNIE: Norman, I'll thump you.

REG: Right. I've got it. Listen. The person with the ball— he calls out somebody's name. And at the same time, he must throw the ball to somebody else. He mustn't throw it to the person whose name he's called out. And he mustn't call his own name. Otherwise, he loses a life. Two lives. And you lose a life if you drop it. Right, here we go. Catch, Tom.

[REG *throws the ball to* ANNIE.]

TOM: [*reacting*] What?

ANNIE: [*catching ball*] Oh. [*She hesitates.*]

REG: Keep it going. You must keep it going fast.

ANNIE: Right. Er—Reg—

[ANNIE *throws the ball to* NORMAN.]

NORMAN: Annie.

[NORMAN *throws to* TOM.]

TOM: Ah. Norman. [TOM *throws to* ANNIE.]

ANNIE: Norman.

[ANNIE *throws to* TOM.]

TOM: Tom—oh no, that's me. Sorry.

REG: Right, that's one life gone.

TOM: Sorry—er—Reg.

[TOM *throws to* ANNIE.]

ANNIE: Tom.

[ANNIE *throws to* NORMAN.]

NORMAN: Annie.

[NORMAN *throws to* REG. REG *drops it.*]

REG: Not too hard. Right, that's one life for me. Annie.

[REG *throws to* NORMAN.]

NORMAN: Annie.

[NORMAN *throws to* TOM.]

TOM: Annie.

[TOM *throws to* ANNIE.]

Oh—sorry—

REG: Out! Right, Tom's out.

TOM: Sorry. I'm no good at this sort of thing. I'll watch.

[*He sits.*]

REG: Annie, come on.

ANNIE: Norman.

[ANNIE *throws to* REG.]

REG: Annie.

[REG *throws to* NORMAN.]

NORMAN: Catch it, Reg.

[NORMAN *throws to* ANNIE. ANNIE *drops it.*]

[*triumphant*] Ha-ha.

[REG *laughs.* ANNIE *looks annoyed.*]

ANNIE: Norman.

[ANNIE *throws to* REG, *who drops it.*]

REG: Steady on, steady on, I wasn't ready.

NORMAN: You were ready, you're out.

REG: No, I wasn't. I wasn't ready. [*To* TOM] You were watching. I wasn't ready, was I?

TOM: Sorry, I missed that.

NORMAN: You're out.

REG: Rubbish.

ANNIE: What happens now?

NORMAN: Just us two.

REG: You can't play with just two of you.

NORMAN: Yes, we can.

REG: Don't be daft—I mean—

NORMAN: [*throwing ball to* ANNIE] Annie.

ANNIE: Norman. [*She throws to him*] This is stupid.

NORMAN: Annie. [*He throws to* ANNIE] No, it isn't.

REG: Oh well, let 'em play if they want to.

[*He sits by* TOM. *Under their ensuing conversation,* NORMAN *and* ANNIE *continue their game—calling each other's name, getting closer and closer together until they are throwing the ball a few inches distance and finally passing it hand to hand.*]

How's that car of yours running?

TOM: Oh, no complaints. No complaints . . .

REG: It's funny because my next door neighbour, he's bought one of those. Same year—same model as yours—he's had a lot of bad luck with his.

TOM: Has he?

REG: He'd done—what?—800 miles, barely run it in. He's starting up this fairly steep hill—in fourth—he changes to third—big lorry behind him, big lorry in front of him—finds he needs to change to second and whack—whole gear lever comes off in his hand. There he is, on this steep hill, stuck in third gear, just about to stall—lorry there—lorry there—could have been nasty.

TOM: Good Lord.

[ANNIE *and* NORMAN, *unseen by them, are now on the ground locked in an embrace.*]

REG: As it happens, luckily, he has the presence of mind to turn his wheel off the road into the ditch.

[RUTH *comes out to collect her handbag which she has left by the chair.*]

Safest place. What else could he do? He said, that's the last time I buy one of those. You won't catch me buying one of those again. You've been lucky up till now, that's all I can say.

RUTH: [*who has been peering at the shape of* NORMAN *and* ANNIE *on the ground for some seconds*] Excuse me, I'm sorry to interrupt, but could you just confirm that I'm seeing what I think I'm seeing?

[REG *and* TOM *turn.*]

REG: Flipping heck.

TOM: [*rising*] Hey! Hey! [*moving to* NORMAN *and* ANNIE] Annie . . . Annie . . .

ANNIE: [*emerging for a second*] Oh, go away.

RUTH: Well, throw a bucket of water over them or something.

TOM: Annie! [*Angry for him*] All right. Two can play at that. Two can play at that. [*He marches up to* RUTH] I love you too. Do you hear, I love you too.

RUTH: I beg your pardon?

TOM: I love you. [*He grabs* RUTH *and kisses her.*]

RUTH: [*struggling furiously*] Tom . . .

[REG *stands between the couples greatly amused.* SARAH *comes out with a tray with one cup on it.*]

SARAH: Now, I'm collecting dirty cups. Are there any—oh, my God. [*She drops her tray*] Tom! Tom! Ruth! Norman! Annie! What are you—? Stop them. Somebody stop them. Reg—

[REG *stands uselessly laughing.*]

Reg, will you do something for once in your life?

Curtain

ACT TWO

Scene Two

The garden. Monday morning 9 a.m. SARAH *and* RUTH *ready to leave.* SARAH *with suitcases packed.*

SARAH: Look at the time. We should be halfway home by now.

RUTH: Sorry to hold you up.

SARAH: It gives you a lot of trouble, does it? Your car?

RUTH: Now and then. It sometimes starts all right. But only if you're not in a hurry to go anywhere.

SARAH: Reg'll get it going.

RUTH: I hope so.

SARAH: It's nice Tom came back this morning.

RUTH: Yes.

SARAH: I'm glad he didn't decide to go off in a huff.

RUTH: No.

SARAH: After yesterday. He could have done.

RUTH: He has a forgiving nature.

SARAH: Yes. But then I suppose one could say that of you.

RUTH: That's one of the hazards of living with Norman. It was much more alarming being attacked by Tom. That I wasn't even expecting.

[REG *enters, jacket off, sleeves up, wiping his hands on a rag.*]

REG: Fuse wire. We need a bit of fuse wire.

SARAH: Look at your hands.

REG: Well, I've been—

SARAH: For heaven's sake, don't get it on your shirt.

REG: [*to* RUTH] It's a very dirty engine you've got there.

RUTH: Sorry. We seldom get round to washing that.

REG: Let alone the outside.

RUTH: It's very kind of you.

REG: No trouble. What I'll do is, I'll bind it on with a bit of fuse wire. It'll only be temporary but it should get you home. She'll still need a shove to start. Could you get it for me?

SARAH: What?

REG: Fuse wire.

SARAH: Why can't you get it?

REG: Well, look at my hands. I'll get it all over everything.

SARAH: Well, I don't see why I—

REG: All right, I'll get it myself. I'll only open the door with my teeth.

SARAH: Oh, I'll get it then. As usual. What is it you want?

REG: Fuse wire. It's usually in the bottom kitchen drawer. That's where we used to keep it. It's very thin, silver coloured wire wrapped round a—

SARAH: I know what fuse wire looks like.

REG: Fine.

SARAH: Wait there. I don't know.

[SARAH *goes*.]

REG: Soon have it fixed.

RUTH: Thank you.

REG: I hope so, anyway. We have to get underway soon or she'll be complaining again. I don't know why we're in such a hurry to get home. I don't have to collect the children till this afternoon. Could have enjoyed the sun. You ought to be at work too, oughtn't you?

RUTH: I think I've just taken the day off. So has Norman.

REG: Ah well, why not?

RUTH: Sarah's being almost amiable towards me at the moment. I don't know why that should be, do you?

REG: No . . .

RUTH: I'm afraid I suspect her when she's nice to me. I don't want to sound mean about your wife but whenever she smiles it usually means some disaster is about to overtake me. She was extremely cheerful on my wedding day, I seem to remember.

REG: Ah.

RUTH: What's she up to? Do you know?

REG: Well . . .

RUTH: What?

REG: It's silly but—er—this sounds ridiculous—but do you think Norman has—er—

RUTH: Has what?

REG: Well—you know. Towards Sarah . . .

RUTH: Norman and Sarah?

REG: No, I don't think he can but . . . I just had this idea. I think I'm just getting jumpy. He's been round everyone else, hasn't he?

RUTH: Everyone else being Annie.

REG: Well, yes. If you like.

RUTH: I don't think you should suspect Norman of everything, you know.

REG: No, no—I just . . .

RUTH: He can't be held responsible for every strange relationship in this family.

REG: No. I'm sorry. I just—

RUTH: He's not a complete monster.

REG: No.

[SARAH *enters with a roll of gardening wire.*]

Ah.

SARAH: There's none there. Only this.

REG: That's garden wire.

SARAH: I know it's garden wire. This is all there is.

REG: Worse than useless. Much too thick.

SARAH: Well, I'm trying to help.

REG: We need fuse wire. I'll find it, don't worry.

SARAH: I've just said there isn't any.

REG: Of course there is. I'll find it.

SARAH: You won't you know.

REG: Want a bet?

SARAH: Why do you always want to make me out a liar?

REG: You missed it. It's there.

SARAH: All right, I'll show you. It isn't there.

REG: It's there.

SARAH: It is not there.

REG: It's always there.

[SARAH *and* REG *have gone.* RUTH *sits.* NORMAN *enters.*]

NORMAN: Where's the man with the fuse wire then?

RUTH: Arguing with his wife, surprisingly. They can't find it.

NORMAN: Oh.

RUTH: Would that have anything to do with you?

NORMAN: Me? I haven't got the fuse wire.

RUTH: I mean, them arguing.

NORMAN: Glad we're staying at home today.

RUTH: I don't think my office will be particularly.

NORMAN: We'll have a great time. Let's do something fun.

RUTH: We could wash up.

NORMAN: No.

RUTH: There's about two months' worth.

NORMAN: No. That's not fun.

RUTH: You could cut our hedge. That man next door complained again. He said he's writing to the council.

NORMAN: Stupid git. Why doesn't he move?

RUTH: That's what he said about us.

NORMAN: It's very cruel to cut hedges. Tell him it's against my principles.

RUTH: You tell him. So you haven't been making eyes at Sarah?

NORMAN: Sarah?

RUTH: In case you'd left anyone out.

NORMAN: Good God. What do you take me for?

RUTH: I took you for a husband, Norman. Very foolishly. I can feel my life expectancy shortening minute by minute. After this weekend, it's down by five years.

NORMAN: Don't blame me. I haven't done anything.

RUTH: What?

NORMAN: Tom's happy. He's forgiven me.

RUTH: Tom is an idiot.

NORMAN: He's a shrewd man. He realized it wasn't serious, Annie and me. Just a mad idea. We were both depressed. I wanted to cheer her up, that's all.

RUTH: Well, next time, send her a funny postcard.

NORMAN: There won't be a next time. I'm concentrating on you.

RUTH: Oh God.

NORMAN: I'll be sorry to leave. I like it down here. Must have been nice to grow up in this house. Was it nice?

RUTH: All right. I'd nothing against the house. It was the people I didn't care for.

NORMAN: You don't know when you're well off. When I think of my childhood, little pokey back to back terrace—

RUTH: Overlooking Regent's Park.

NORMAN: Hyde Park.

RUTH: Well . . .

NORMAN: The unfashionable side. The slums of South Kensington. They were hard days, lass. Anyway, Hyde Park's not country. It's just an underground car park with a grass roof. Shall we have a party tonight?

RUTH: No, we won't.

NORMAN: Go on. That'd be fun.

RUTH: I'm much too tired.

NORMAN: Right. We'll go to bed. We'll go to bed.

RUTH: I said I'm tired.

NORMAN: To rest. We'll rest.

RUTH: I know you and your rests. Your mind just doesn't associate beds with sleep at all. I don't know when you do sleep. It certainly isn't with me.

NORMAN: I was brought up to believe it was very insulting to sleep with your wife or any lady. A gentleman stays eagerly awake. He sleeps at his work. That's what work's for. Why do you think they have the S I L E N C E notices in the library? So as not to disturb me in my little nook behind the biography shelves. L-P.

RUTH: They'll sack you.

NORMAN: They daren't. I reorganized the Main Index. When I die, the secret dies with me.

[TOM *enters.*]

TOM: Well, that's done it.

NORMAN: Done what?

TOM: The thing on your car. I've fixed it back on.

NORMAN: I thought we needed wire.

TOM: No. It screwed on. Don't need wire.

NORMAN: This vet is a genius.

TOM: No. The same thing happened on mine. They're always falling off, those things.

NORMAN: Brilliant.

RUTH: Do you think someone should tell Reg? He's still hunting for wire, you know.

TOM: Oh, good Lord, is he? I'd better tell him.

NORMAN: No. Let me—

TOM: It's all right, I'll—

NORMAN: Please. Let me. I want to see his face . . .

[NORMAN *goes off gleefully.*]

RUTH: He's so bouncy this morning, I could kick him.

TOM: Yes. Well—er . . .

RUTH: Oh, do stop looking like that, Tom.

TOM: What?

RUTH: Embarrassed and furtive.

TOM: Well, I was just—

RUTH: Forget all about it. It was a misunderstanding.

TOM: I don't usually grab hold of women in that way, you know.

RUTH: I do realize.

TOM: I don't want you to get the impression I—

RUTH: I haven't.

TOM: As long as you appreciate . . .

[*Pause.*]

RUTH: It's a pity you don't, in a way.

TOM: What?

RUTH: Grab hold a bit more.

TOM: How do you mean?

RUTH: Annie, for instance. She might even appreciate it.

TOM: Oh, I don't think so. I don't think she goes in for that sort of thing.

RUTH: Apart from with Norman.

TOM: Ah. [*Pause*] That's a good point. Hadn't looked at it quite like that.

RUTH: I think you should.

TOM: Women are really dreadfully complicated, aren't they? Or do I mean human beings?

RUTH: They can be one and the same.

TOM: I mean, with other animals, well the majority of them, they're either off heat or on heat. Everyone knows where they are. I probably should have been born a horse or something. With Annie, I never really know. I mean, just now I was chatting away with her about something or other—she started breaking a plate.

RUTH: What?

TOM: Smashing a plate. No reason. Just simply smashing a plate. I hardly like to say anything to her, when she's like that. In case she starts on me.

RUTH: I think she might, shortly.

[REG *comes out angrily.* NORMAN *follows, gleeful.*]

REG: [*to* TOM] Well, thank you very much.

TOM: That's all right.

REG: You might have told me it screwed. I've wasted half an hour looking for fuse wire that isn't where it should be.

TOM: Sorry. I thought you knew it screwed.

REG: If I'd known it screwed, I wouldn't—and this herbert isn't much help, sniggering away.

RUTH: Norman, stop sniggering.

NORMAN: I am not sniggering. These are joyful guffaws.

REG: Did you put the top on again?

TOM: No. I thought you might want to—

REG: Right. Norman.

NORMAN: What?

REG: Come and do something useful for once.

NORMAN: If it's only for once.

REG: We'll put it together. I'll tow you as far as the top of the hill and then you can roll her down, Ruth. That should start her. Oh. One moment. Have I got my tow rope? I don't think I have. I think I took it out to make room for the cases. Do you carry a tow rope?

NORMAN: No idea. We've lost the key of the boot.

REG: How do you open it?

RUTH: We haven't, for months.

REG: Oh, grief . . .

[ANNIE *comes out.*]

NORMAN: My gym shoes are in there, too.

REG: Annie.

NORMAN: And my football.

ANNIE: Hallo.

NORMAN: Never mind, it will rust away eventually.

REG: Annie, have we got such a thing as a rope? Big thick one.

ANNIE: I think there's one in the cellar. It's very heavy.

REG: Just the job. Tom.

TOM: Um?

REG: You fetch the rope.

TOM: Rope?

ANNIE: It's in the cellar. Foot of the steps.

TOM: Oh. Right. Rope.

[*He goes.*]

REG: Norman, follow me.

[*He strides off.*]

NORMAN: [*following* REG] Must be marvellous to be a leader of men.

[NORMAN *goes off.*]

RUTH: I think we're going to spend another night here at this rate.

ANNIE: Oh well, it's no bother.

RUTH: I think it's better if we don't. This country air has a disastrous effect on some of us. Not that I blame anyone particularly. Least of all you. Looking after that woman's enough to turn you completely.

ANNIE: I'm sorry. I've said I'm sorry.

RUTH: Why should you be? It was entirely Norman's fault.

ANNIE: Not really. I was feeling lonely and sorry for myself and—

RUTH: Yes, I'm sure you were. That doesn't excuse Norman.

ANNIE: He was lonely too.

RUTH: Norman? Nonsense. What's Norman got to be lonely about? Sorry for himself maybe. No, he just can't bear not to be the centre of attention. Anyway, we won't talk about Norman. He gets talked about enough. Which is why he does these things in the first place. You and Tom. . .

ANNIE: Yes.

RUTH: Do try and sort out something between you, will you? You can't let it drag on and on. It's really absurd. You both want to get together, you both should. Look it's a lovely day. As soon as we've all gone, sit Tom down out here and tell him point blank, either he marries you or comes and lives with you, or whatever it is you both want, or else he clears off for good. That'll do it. Be so much more convenient. And then we wouldn't have to worry about you.

ANNIE: Which would also be convenient.

RUTH: Well, we do worry and there's no point in you giving up everything for Mother's sake. You'll turn into a martyr like Sarah which would be too dreadful for words. Two of you in the family.

ANNIE: Don't worry.

RUTH: You can't sit around smashing crockery for the rest of your life. It's sometimes quite satisfying but it's no substitute for the real thing.

ANNIE: Who told you about that?

RUTH: Tom.

ANNIE: Oh.

RUTH: Who else?

ANNIE: No one.

[SARAH comes out, holding fuse wire.]

SARAH: There. Fuse wire. It wasn't where he said at all. I

knew it wasn't. He wouldn't believe me till he'd seen for himself. Do you know where I found it?

ANNIE: In the pantry on the second shelf.

SARAH: Fancy keeping it in the pantry. Who on earth keeps fuse wire in a pantry?

ANNIE: People who have fuse boxes in their pantry.

SARAH: Look at the time. Where is he then? I'd better give this to him.

RUTH: I wouldn't bother.

SARAH: Why?

RUTH: He doesn't need it.

SARAH: Doesn't need it? What do you mean, he doesn't need it?

[REG enters.]

REG: Now then.

SARAH: What do you mean you don't need it?

REG: Need what?

SARAH: This fuse wire you've been going on about.

REG: Oh, we fixed that hours ago.

SARAH: Do you realize that I have been—?

REG: We couldn't wait all day for you, could we? Right. We're ready to go.

ANNIE: What about your rope?

REG: Ah. I had it. Had it all the time. Thought I'd taken it out but I hadn't.

[NORMAN enters.]

NORMAN: All knots secured, skipper.

RUTH: Has he tied the tow rope?

REG: Yes.

RUTH: Check it.

NORMAN: What do you mean? We old nautical men. I'll have you know I've crossed the Serpentine in my day. Couldn't do it now, blast it. Not with this old peg leg.

RUTH: Come on, Norman.

REG: I'll tow you as far as the top of the hill, right? We'll disconnect the rope and then you're free to roll her down. But for heaven's sake wait till I'm out of the way.

NORMAN: This could be fun.

SARAH: Come along, we're very late. Goodbye Annie. Thank you for—looking after us . . .

ANNIE: You're welcome.

REG: [*gathering up the cases*] See you at Christmas. If not before.

SARAH: I shouldn't think before.

REG: No, no. Well . . .

RUTH: Bye bye, Annie.

ANNIE: Bye.

NORMAN: Take care.

ANNIE: Yes.

SARAH: Bye.

[*All except* ANNIE *start to leave.*]

REG: [*as they go*] Now keep your hand brake on till I give you the word. I don't want you rolling into the back of me.

RUTH: All right, all right . . .

[*They go.* ANNIE *watches them out of sight. She turns back to the house.* NORMAN *darts on again.*]

NORMAN: [*an urgent whisper*] Annie! Annie!

ANNIE: Norman. What are you—?

NORMAN: Just came to say goodbye.

ANNIE: Oh Norman, you're—

NORMAN: I'll give you a ring. Can I?

ANNIE: Yes, If you—

NORMAN: Next time I'll plan it a bit better, Annie. I promise. I'll fix it well in advance—so that—

ANNIE: Norman . . .

NORMAN: What?

ANNIE: We can't.

NORMAN: Of course we can. You'd like to wouldn't you? Wouldn't you?

ANNIE: Yes, but . . .

NORMAN: I'll fix it. Don't worry.

ANNIE: You said that last time. Look what happened. We upset everybody. Ruth, Tom, Sarah.

NORMAN: We love each other, don't we?

ANNIE: [*wearily*] I don't know.

NORMAN: You'd be happy with me, wouldn't you? You'd be happy?

ANNIE: Yes.

NORMAN: [*moving to embrace her*] Oh, Annie . . . oh God. [*He is entangled in the brambles*] These damn things again.

ANNIE: All right. Keep still. Keep still.

NORMAN: Oh, Annie . . . ow!

ANNIE: There we are.

[*Car horn.*]

NORMAN: I don't want to lose you, Annie.

ANNIE: They're waiting.

NORMAN: I won't lose you, will I, Annie?

ANNIE: Not if you don't want to . . .

NORMAN: I don't. I really don't.

[*Two car horns in unison.*]

ANNIE: Go on, Norman, go on.

NORMAN: Goodbye. I love you. Goodbye.

[NORMAN *goes off blowing kisses back to her.*]

ANNIE: Oh, Norman . . .

[*She stands for a second.* TOM *comes out laden with a very heavy coil of rope.*]

TOM: Here we are. Is this the one? [*Looking around*] Oh. Where are they?

ANNIE: They've gone.

TOM: They'll need this.

ANNIE: They've got one.

TOM: Oh. Wasted journey.

ANNIE: Yes.

TOM: Oh well . . . [*He stands, the rope still on his shoulder, where it remains throughout the scene*] Peace and quiet again, eh?

ANNIE: Yes.

TOM: Quite a weekend.

ANNIE: Yes.

TOM: I must say, I'm rather relieved Ruth's gone. After my incident. Bit embarrassing.

ANNIE: Yes.

TOM: Expect you're glad to see the back of Norman, aren't you? For the same reason. Yes. You must be. [*Pause.*] Look. Annie . . .

ANNIE: Mmm?

TOM: I've been piecing things together in my mind—fitting the various bits to fill in the picture—building a sort of overall view of things—so I can more or less get an objective angle on it and—er—well, I expect you know what I'm going to say next . . .?

ANNIE: Honestly, Tom, I couldn't begin to guess.

TOM: Oh. Was rather hoping you might. Made it all a bit— save me a—it's a shame we're not horses.

ANNIE: What are you talking about, Tom?

TOM: Well. It seems to me—that we ought to find a way of —well—sorting out our relationship—if we have one—to such a degree that we—come together more or less on a permanent basis. Temporarily at least.

ANNIE: Are you talking about marriage?

TOM: Yes.

ANNIE: Oh.

TOM: And no.

ANNIE: Which is it?

TOM: Well, it could be a lot looser . . .

ANNIE: As loose as we are now, you mean?

TOM: No. I meant a bit tighter than that. Somewhere in between. Well, loose and tight. The whole hog if you want to. It's up to you.

ANNIE: I see.

TOM: What do you say?

[*A silence.*]

Annie . . .

[*A silence.*]

Would you like me to marry you? I would. Like me to marry you. May I? I want to.

ANNIE: [*at length*] I don't know.

TOM: Oh.

ANNIE: I'll see.

TOM: Oh. I got the idea that perhaps that's what you would have liked.

ANNIE: I did, I think. I'm sorry, Tom, you'll have to wait.

TOM: How long for?

ANNIE: At least until I've had a chance to—go away somewhere. And think about it.

TOM: Oh, I see. Fair enough.

[*Pause.*]

Going to be a scorcher today, again.

ANNIE: Yes.

TOM: Far too nice to do any work. It's on days like this you really feel at peace with the world. That's what I feel . . .

[*Two loud horns. A distant crash of colliding vehicles.*]

[*recovering*] Good grief.

ANNIE: It's them.

TOM: Hang on. Stay there. Stay there—this could be nasty.

ANNIE: Quickly, we must . . .

[*She starts to move away.*]

TOM: [*pulling her back*] No, please, Annie—stay there. Stay there.

[TOM *rushes off.* ANNIE *stands anxiously.*]

REG: [*off*] You bloody fool.

[REG *stamps on followed by* RUTH *and* SARAH. SARAH *flustered.* NORMAN *follows up the rear with* TOM.]

REG: What the hell did you let him drive for?

RUTH: He insisted.

TOM: Everyone all right?

REG: Why him? Why him?

SARAH: I feel terribly faint.

NORMAN: You can't expect Ruth to drive.

REG: Why not?

NORMAN: She hasn't got her glasses.

REG: She could drive better than you blindfolded. Where were your brakes?

TOM: Any casualties?

SARAH: I feel giddy.

REG: I told you distinctly. Wait till I'm out of the way.

NORMAN: My mistake.

REG: Your mistake? You weren't even in gear.

SARAH: I need a glass of water.

TOM: I'm not a doctor but I am a vet. If anyone needs any treatment.

ANNIE: Is there much damage?

NORMAN: Yes, we smashed his whole back end in.

REG: I know you've smashed the whole back end in. The damn cars are twisted together like bloody spaghetti.

SARAH: I've never been so shaken.

RUTH: Sit down, Sarah.

ANNIE: Do you want to phone? Phone the *AA*?

REG: Some people have as much sense as a—you won't get home today, you know that?

SARAH: Well, we'll stay, dear, we'll stay.

REG: I'll have to phone home as well. Somebody get the cases out. I'll do the phoning. [*To* RUTH] Why did you let him drive? You know what he's like. You knew he was Norman, didn't you?

[REG *goes indoors.*]

NORMAN: My mistake.

TOM: I'll start fetching the cases, shall I?

SARAH: Thank you. Tom. I'm so shaky, I—

TOM: You stay there.

SARAH: I will.

TOM: Everyone stay there. Reg and I have got it under control.

[TOM *goes off.*]

NORMAN: Definitely my mistake . . .

[*A silence.*]

[NORMAN *stands regarding the three women who are now seated. They look at him.*]

Well. Back again.

ANNIE: Oh, Norman . . .

RUTH: If I didn't know you better, I'd say you did all that deliberately.

NORMAN: Me? Why should I want to do that?

SARAH: Huh.

NORMAN: Give me one good reason why I'd do a thing like that?

RUTH: Offhand, I can think of three.

[*Pause.*]

NORMAN: Ah. [*Brightening*] Well, since we're all here, we ought to make the most if it, eh? What do you say?

[NORMAN *smiles round at the women in turn.* RUTH *gets up and without another word, goes.*]

[*After her*] Ruth . . .

[*He turns to* ANNIE *but she too has risen and is going.*]

Annie . . .

[*He turns to* SARAH. *She likewise, rises and leaves.*]

Sarah!

[NORMAN *is left alone, bewildered, then genuinely hurt and indignant.*]

[*Shouting after them*] I only wanted to make you happy.

Curtain